Laura's List

Laura's List

The First Lady's List of 57 Great Books
for Families and Children

Beverly Darnall

JEREMY P. TARCHER/PENGUIN

a member of Penguin Group (USA) Inc.

New York

JEREMY P. TARCHER/PENGUIN
Published by the Penguin Group

Penguin Group (USA) Inc., 375 Hudson Street, New York, New York 10014, USA • Penguin Group (Canada), 90 Eglinton Avenue East, Suite 700, Toronto, Ontario M4P 2Y3, Canada (a division of Pearson Penguin Canada Inc.) • Penguin Books Ltd, 80 Strand, London WC2R 0RL, England • Penguin Group Ireland, 25 St Stephen's Green, Dublin 2, Ireland (a division of Penguin Books Ltd) • Penguin Group (Australia), 250 Camberwell Road, Camberwell, Victoria 3124, Australia (a division of Pearson Australia Group Pty Ltd) • Penguin Books India Pvt Ltd, 11 Community Centre, Panchsheel Park, New Delhi–110 017, India • Penguin Group (NZ), Cnr Airborne and Rosedale Roads, Albany, Auckland 1310, New Zealand (a division of Pearson New Zealand Ltd) • Penguin Books (South Africa) (Pty) Ltd, 24 Sturdee Avenue, Rosebank, Johannesburg 2196, South Africa

Penguin Books Ltd, Registered Offices: 80 Strand, London WC2R 0RL, England

Most Tarcher/Penguin books are available at special quantity discounts for bulk purchase for sales promotions, premiums, fund-raising, and educational needs. Special books or book excerpts also can be created to fit specific needs. For details, write Penguin Group (USA) Inc. Special Markets, 375 Hudson Street, New York, NY 10014.

An application has been submitted to register this book with the Library of Congress.

ISBN 1-58542-503-6

Printed in the United States of America
1   3   5   7   9   10   8   6   4   2

This book is printed on acid-free paper. ∞

Book design by Meighan Cavanaugh

While the author has made every effort to provide accurate telephone numbers and Internet addresses at the time of publication, neither the publisher nor the author assumes any responsibility for errors, or for changes that occur after publication. Further, the publisher does not have any control over and does not assume any responsibility for author or third-party websites or their content.

For Isaac and Joel

From your parents you learn love and laughter and how to put one foot before the other.
But when books are opened you discover that you have wings.

HELEN HAYES (1900–1993)

A truly great book should be read in youth, again in maturity, and once more in old age,
as a fine building should be seen by morning light, at noon, and by moonlight.

ROBERTSON DAVIES (1913–1995)

I started reading, I read everything I could get my hands on. . . . By the time
I was thirteen I had read myself out of Harlem.

JAMES BALDWIN (1924–1987)

A home without books is like a room without windows.

HENRY WARD BEECHER (1813–1887)

Contents

Family Reading

Books to Read to and with Young Children

Books for Intermediate and Independent Readers

Special Comfort Books

Acknowledgments

It was my immense pleasure to spend dozens of days in the beautiful main branch of the Nashville Public Library while writing this book, and I am thankful for the kind help of its librarians and staff. I would like to thank Karen Dean Fry for planting the idea for this book in my mind. I extend my gratitude to Mitch Horowitz for thinking it was a worthy undertaking, to Chartwell Literary Group for facilitating the project, and to Ronn Huff Jr., and Merrill Farnsworth for their hard work. I would especially like to acknowledge and thank Stephen Mansfield, whose skill and excellence as a writer are a constant inspiration to me. His encouragement made this project possible.

Introduction

The idea of writing about the books Laura Bush recommends for families appealed to me from the moment a friend first suggested it. I already knew that Mrs. Bush is more than just another public figure pushing literacy. She is a professional in her own right: a thoughtful educator, an experienced librarian, and a literary expert. I knew her recommendations would be carefully chosen and interesting. I also suspected her suggestions would reflect her own character. She is, after all, a woman of great grace and poise for whom I have tremendous admiration. Still, I could not have known what a treat was in store for me.

When it was time to get to work, I went to the library and started checking out the titles on what I began to call *Laura's List*. Soon every surface in my office was covered with stacks of children's books, and I have to admit it was a pretty cheerful scene. All those colors, those wonderful pictures—just walking into the room made me smile. And it wasn't just the covers that lit up my world. The stories moved me. The characters became real to me. In great children's literature there is a wealth of meaning and values, of humor and honesty, and I had forgotten what a bright influence these stories can have.

The experience took me back to those sweet years when my son and I would often read together. Isaac did not have brothers and sisters in the house when he was growing up and I had a flexible work schedule. This allowed for many hours of reading together. In fact, some of my best memories are of cold winter days by the fire with my little boy, a good book, and two cups of tea. Isaac took books pretty seriously even then, often reading them aloud to his dog or dragging them up into his favorite tree. He's in college now, studying English in hopes of being a teacher. Clearly, early reading of great literature profoundly affected his life. We still discuss the things we are reading and take advantage of long hours on car trips by listening to books on CD.

Returning to the world of great books for children after all these years has also reminded me of my own childhood. I was the seventh of seven children and my home was a busy, crowded place as far removed from my son's experience as it could be. Still, books had a deep impact on my life. I retreated with them often and found in them a doorway to thought and imagination. Books opened my mind to the world and helped me fashion a picture of possibilities, a picture that inspired me and urged me on.

As I began working on *Laura's List,* I became even more keenly aware of how much the children of our video generation need to be introduced early to the world of books. Reading awakens imagination and guides thought in a way that television and movies never can. It creates intellectual passion and a capacity to envision that leads to creativity and a thrilling life of the mind. Reading also has the power to transform a home. It not only creates a lasting bond between child and parent, it can make a home a haven from the commotion of frantic schedules and noise that is modern life. Thought becomes possible, conversations thrive, and home becomes a place of nurturing the soul. These experiences leave a lasting mark on the heart of a child and are cherished even more in adulthood.

The beauty of this vision is that it is within easy grasp of every American. No matter who you are or where you live, no matter what your income, you can give your child the beautiful, essential gift of books. Used and new books can be bought in stores and online; many times the classics are available for a dollar or two. There are libraries in every town, and library cards are free. Books have almost become a birthright in America today.

Still, not all books are great and not all are worth reading. You will need a guide to lead you to treasure. Laura Bush has already offered one and you now hold it in your hands. I hope you will find *Laura's List* to be a gateway to the fascinating universe of reading for you and your child.

Laura Bush: A Brief Biography

Without question, Laura Bush leads an extraordinary life. As the wife of the President of the United States, she meets famous and fascinating people, travels all over the world, and sees the inner workings of the events of our time from a unique vantage point. Within the space of just a few months, her schedule might require that she crisscross the continent and then circle the globe giving speeches and shaking hands. It is not an experience most of us will ever have or even come close to having, and it is certainly not the life Laura Welch envisioned when she was a child.

Hers was a typical American upbringing. She was raised in a West Texas town by a father who was a real-estate developer and a mother who worked as his secretary. Laura grew up in a peaceful, secure home with loving attention and plenty of friends. Her life had the other usual ingredients—days in class at the neighborhood school, church every Sunday, and Girl Scout meetings. As an only child, Laura had many hours to herself and she could usually be found somewhere with her nose in a book. That's where it all started, this passion for literature that she still carries today.

Much of who Laura Bush is came from her life with books. Before she was the First Lady of Texas or the First Lady of the United States, she was a teacher and a librarian. And before that, she was a little girl who loved to read.

As Laura Bush said at a 2005 awards ceremony, "I first fell in love with books when I was a child in Midland, Texas. My mother used to take me to the Midland County Public Library, which was in the basement of the courthouse in the center of the town I grew up in. And we'd check out books, and then we would spend hours reading with each other. I was an only child, but I soon found that I didn't have to be lonely as long as I had a book in my hand."

Clearly, for Laura, the library was a favorite destination. "I am fortunate that my mother took me to get my library card at an early age. In fact, that was the first card I carried in my wallet," Mrs. Bush once said, "and I used it throughout my childhood to borrow books from what seemed to me to be a vast and inexhaustible collection."

Not surprisingly, Laura loved school, and she particularly admired her second-grade teacher, Mrs. Gnagy. She decided when she was seven years old that she wanted to be just like her. Even when she was ready to graduate from high school, she still remembered the influence of this beloved teacher and decided to follow in her footsteps. Laura enrolled in Southern Methodist University and graduated with a bachelor's degree in education. After teaching for three years in the Texas public schools, she decided to be more specific in her focus, and went on to earn a master of library science degree from the University of Texas. She spent the next few years doing what she loved best. As a librarian she could offer her students the gift that had been so precious to her as a child: a love for reading.

Marrying George W. Bush changed all that. Her husband's path took her out of the library and eventually into the White House, but her commitment to the care and education of children has never diminished. She champions many causes that focus on literature and learning (see a list of Mrs. Bush's causes in the back of this book), and one of her great pleasures is a visit to an elementary school for a read-aloud session with the lucky students. She holds a book up so even the smallest child can see it and then begins to read. Listening to her point out the pictures and engage the children, I find it obvious that she was a great teacher and a wonderful librarian. Her enthusiasm for the story and her interest in the little listeners are her only focus.

Laura Bush has expertise in the larger world of literature as well. She is often asked which authors are her favorites. The list is varied and interesting: Edith Wharton, Fyodor Dostoyevsky, Anthony Doerr, Ian McEwan, David Lindsey, Willa Cather, Mary Oliver, E. B. White, and Ray Bradbury, to name a few. She reads broadly: historical fiction, biographies, and novels. And then there is the wonderful list of authors celebrated in a series she hosts at the White House: Truman Capote, Flannery O'Connor, Eudora Welty, Mark Twain, Langston Hughes, Edna Ferber, and others, not to mention the contemporary authors, like Bret Lott, Elizabeth Spencer, and Tom Wolfe, who lead the discussions. She undoubtedly relishes this pearl of an opportunity to bring such talent together.

It has been noted that Mrs. Bush has a knowledge of literature that is often astonishing to the authors, editors, professors, and publishers she invites to the White House. In a 2003 *Business Week* article, "Laura Bush, Your Country Needs You," Thane Peterson calls her gift for organizing literary programs a "Texas-size surprise," and remarks, "She's one of the most literate people associated with any White House in decades." Her mastery of literature should not come as such a surprise. After all, she's only the second First Lady to have completed a graduate degree. Perhaps the fact that her achievements are not well known can be explained by another facet of Laura Bush's personality. As one columnist has noted, she is "strikingly unvain and downright uncooperative" when it comes to discussing her own accomplishments. She is more than willing to use her position to promote what she knows are worthwhile causes, but she doesn't use it to promote herself.

Mrs. Bush's reticence to tout her own achievements is largely due to the fact that, at heart, she is a normal American woman. She has had to learn to pick out designer gowns, but she is most comfortable in jeans and a T-shirt. She dines with princes and celebrities, but still prefers to spend what extra time she has with friends from childhood and college. She dislikes the title "First Lady," asking her staff to call her "Laura Bush" or "Mrs. Bush." She works in an unpretentious office with children's books on the shelves rather than in a highly decorated space. She seems down-to-earth and elegant at the same time, and Americans love her for it. Her approval rating has been consistently high—85 percent at one time, according to a Gallup poll. The citizens of this country respect her and relate to her. More important, they sense that she relates to them. Many American wives, mothers, and daughters feel that the same things that matter to them matter to Laura Bush. As Hanna Rosin, a *Washington Post* staff writer, stated in an essay, "If you are in the audience in your business suit, she's speaking to you. If you're pushing the stroller, she's speaking to you. She's not Jackie O, and she's not Hillary. She's just a reflection of you."

Laura Bush's life with books has done much to make her the unique individual she is. Her reading has exposed her to a wealth of experience far beyond even what her extraordinary life offers. Books broaden the mind but keep the soul connected to the value of everyday life. Mrs. Bush is a gracious woman who knows the weight of big issues and still cares about the little things. She is familiar with the thoughts of great writers, and also knows the value of ordinary moments. That is why the books that she recommends are worth considering.

Laura Bush brings such depth to her book recommendations because she has the heart of a mother, the skills of a librarian, and the determination of a true educator. It is a powerful combination. Her university degrees required that she develop a professional perspective on children's literature. That means she not only considers how a book affects families and children on a surface level, but evaluates books with the skill of a specialist. It comes as no surprise, then, that Laura's List is filled with books that illuminate every aspect of a child's life. She chose books that would provide assurance and feelings of security at bedtime, books that have proven over and over again to demystify the darkness and send a child peacefully to sleep. She included books about being a good friend and unleashing the imagination, stories that encourage cooperation and reward resourcefulness. The reader is introduced to characters that learn to live with loss and find a way to offer forgiveness. She added simple stories of childhoods in the past. Many of the books expand the reader's world with tales from faraway or unfamiliar cultures.

As I read each of the books on Laura's List, I felt as though I was getting a glimpse into the personality of Mrs. Bush. I couldn't help but notice—in fact, it is my purpose in this book to notice—the themes to which she is drawn. I'm sure she chose these books because she feels that they say important things to little ones and open the door for communication between adult and child. If the books on Laura's List are any indication of what she holds dear, it is clear that she has an amazing compassion for those who have been abandoned or suffer loneliness. She celebrates the individual gifts of each person and loves humor.

In Mrs. Bush's choices there is respect for the complex lessons taught by nature. She understands the raw yearning each human has for freedom and knows that nothing teaches this lesson better than the emotional stories of immigrants.

She believes that history and heritage are to be embraced, because in looking back we remember the price paid for the present moment. Through all the stories there is a common thread of basic moral values, such as honesty and generosity. If these books embody the values that are important to her, then we also know that she believes in the sanctuary of family and in the creative, healing force of love.

Laura Bush reveals her passion for literature in the selection of these particular titles for families and children. The books themselves are a testimony to her long dedication to the liberating, enlightening world of words.

How to Make the Best Use of Laura's List

This book is based on Laura Bush's recommended reading list for children and families. The list can be found on the White House Web site (whitehouse.gov/firstlady). I have chosen to preserve the order and organization that Mrs. Bush used in presenting her list.

The books on Laura's List are categorized in the following way:

Family reading
Books to read to and with young children
Books for intermediate and independent readers

In this book, each of the fifty-seven books on Laura's List is explored. Each chapter is devoted to one book and includes a synopsis and an excerpt, along with the following helpful information:

- Length of the book
- Age-appropriate guidelines
- A list of the themes found in the book

- Thoughts on the themes found in each book, entitled "The Heart of the Book"
- Advice for enriching your child's reading time, entitled "Reader's Guide"

The best results will be achieved by reading the chapter about a given book before reading the book itself. In this way the reader will be armed with insights and themes to emphasize while reading. The "Dig Deeper" questions provide additional guidance for discussion and reflection.

Laura's List

Family Reading

To be read aloud as a family.
These titles are also good for independent readers.

1. *Charlotte's Web*   E. B. White
2. *Hank the Cowdog* (series)   John R. Erickson
3. *Little House on the Prairie* (series)   Laura Ingalls Wilder
4. *Little Women*   Louisa May Alcott
5. *Old Yeller*   Fred Gipson
6. *The People Could Fly*   Virginia Hamilton
7. *Where the Red Fern Grows*   Wilson Rawls
8. *Winnie-the-Pooh* (series)   A. A. Milne

Books to Read to and with Young Children

These titles are also good for early independent readers
and those children just learning to read.

9. *Goodnight Moon*   Margaret Wise Brown
10. *Babar* (series)   Jean de Brunhoff and Laurent de Brunhoff
11. *Carlo Likes Reading*   Jessica Spanyol

12. *Clifford, the Big Red Dog* (series)   Norman Bridwell

13. *Corduroy*   Don Freeman

14. *Frances the Badger* (series)   Russell Hoban

15. *Hop on Pop*   Dr. Seuss

16. *Make Way for Ducklings*   Robert McCloskey

17. *Mother Goose Rhymes*

18. *Nana Upstairs & Nana Downstairs*   Tomie dePaola

19. *The Very Hungry Caterpillar*   Eric Carle

20. *There Was an Old Lady Who Swallowed a Fly*   Simms Taback

21. *Where the Wild Things Are*   Maurice Sendak

22. *Why Mosquitoes Buzz in People's Ears*   Verna Aardema

23. *Cars and Trucks and Things That Go*   Richard Scarry

24. *Cuadros de Familia /Family Pictures*   Carmen Lomas Garza

25. *Curious George*   H. A. Rey

26. *Frog and Toad* (series)   Arnold Lobel

27. *George and Martha* (series)   James Marshall

28. *If You Give a Pig a Pancake*   Laura Numeroff

29. *Little Bear* (series)   Else Holmelund Minarik

30. *Magda's Tortillas*   Becky Chavarría-Cháirez

31. *Officer Buckle and Gloria*   Peggy Rathmann

32. *Sarah's Flag for Texas*   Jane Alexander Knapik

33. *Sylvester and the Magic Pebble*   William Steig

34. *The Snowy Day*   Ezra Jack Keats

35. *The Wind in the Willows*   Kenneth Grahame

36. *Tomás and the Library Lady*   Pat Mora

37. *Amazing Grace*   Mary Hoffman

Books for Intermediate and Independent Readers

38. *Esperanza Rising*   Pam Muñoz Ryan

39. *Love That Dog*   Sharon Creech

40. *A Year Down Yonder*   Richard Peck

41. *Because of Winn-Dixie*   Kate DiCamillo
42. *Adaline Falling Star*   Mary Pope Osborne
43. *Joey Pigza Loses Control*   Jack Gantos
44. *Journey to the River Sea*   Eva Ibbotson
45. *Bridge to Terabithia*   Katherine Paterson
46. *Miracle's Boys*   Jacqueline Woodson
47. *Where the Sidewalk Ends*   Shel Silverstein
48. *Homeless Bird*   Gloria Whelan
49. *James and the Giant Peach*   Roald Dahl
50. *Sarah, Plain and Tall*   Patricia MacLachlan
51. *Ramona* (series)   Beverly Cleary
52. *A Wrinkle in Time*   Madeleine L'Engle
53. *My Side of the Mountain*   Jean Craighead George
54. *Tuck Everlasting*   Natalie Babbitt

Special Comfort Books

55. *The Story About Ping*   Marjorie Flack and Kurt Wiese
56. *The Tenth Good Thing About Barney*   Judith Viorst
57. *I Love You, Little One*   Nancy Tafuri

Family Reading

1.

Charlotte's Web

BY E. B. WHITE

Illustrated by Garth Williams

190 pages, 3 to 4 hours of reading time
Ages 8 to 12

THEMES
friendship, death, heroism, justice,
family, creativity, growing up

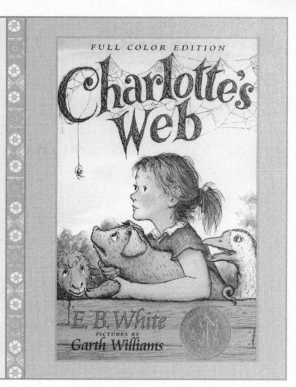

The Story

Poor Wilbur the pig. He was born a runt, and runts aren't much use on a farm. When Fern Arable learns that her father is planning to kill Wilbur because he's not worth keeping, she adopts the little piglet as her own and nurses him until he gets big enough to go to his new home on her uncle's farm. She tries to visit him every day, but when her trips to the barn become less frequent, Wilbur gets lonely and depressed. The goose doesn't have time for him, and Templeton, the bad-tempered, self-centered rat, is not much of a friend at all. Even Wilbur's scary foray out into the big world is a mistake. "If this is what it is like to be free," he thought, "I believe I'd rather be penned up in my own yard."

That's when he meets the best friend any pig could ever find: Charlotte, the gray spider. She reaches out to him when he is lonely and they become fast friends. The days are beautiful and life is good in the barnyard, where the animals talk to one another (and special children understand them), until Wilbur finds out he is destined to become crispy bacon and baked ham on the farmhouse dinner table. Charlotte dreams up a scheme for saving Wilbur, a miracle indeed, and everyone finds out that even though there is sadness in loss and nothing stays the same, friendship is the richest part of life.

A Page from *Charlotte's Web*

When Mr. Arable returned to the house half an hour later, he carried a carton under his arm. Fern was upstairs changing her sneakers. The kitchen table was set for breakfast, and the room smelled of coffee, bacon, damp plaster, and wood smoke from the stove. "Put it on her chair!" said Mrs. Arable. Mr. Arable set the carton down at Fern's place. Then he walked to the sink and washed his hands and dried them on the roller towel.

Fern came slowly down the stairs. Her eyes were red from crying. As she approached her chair, the carton wobbled, and there was a scratching noise. Fern looked at her father. Then she lifted the lid of the carton. There, inside, looking up at her, was the newborn pig. It was a white one. The morning light shone through its ears, turning them pink.

"He's yours," said Mr. Arable. "Saved from an untimely death. And may the good Lord forgive me for this foolishness."

Fern couldn't take her eyes off the tiny pig. "Oh," she whispered. "Oh, look at him! He's absolutely perfect."

The Heart of the Book

It is true that most people have never heard a conversation between a sheep and a spider, nor seen a rat tie a string to a pig's tail. These are easy things to imagine in *Charlotte's Web* because the personalities are recognizable and the emotions are real.

✸ *friendship*

Charlotte is the best kind of friend to Wilbur. She just likes him, and that grows into love, and that love makes her want to help him. She doesn't expect anything from him, and he is perplexed by her willing sacrifices. "Why did you do all this for me?" he asks. "I don't deserve it. I've never done anything for you." When he is finally able to do something in return, he does not hesitate. She has taught him what real friendship is.

✸ *death*

It's natural that Wilbur's owner plans to take him to the slaughterhouse. After all, farmers raise animals for food. Nevertheless, Wilbur is understandably terrified at the prospect, and it takes a very talented spider to help him avoid the ax. The very sensitive subject of death is handled in a gentle but straightforward way in *Charlotte's Web*. Children can discover that death comes to every creature, that it is normal to fear it, but that it is an inevitable part of life. Wilbur cannot keep Charlotte from dying, but he can keep her memory with him after she is gone.

✸ *heroism*

Never was there a more unlikely hero than Charlotte. The small gray spider has only her wits and her compassion as weapons, but she comes to Wilbur's rescue time and again, and her love and ingenuity save him in the end. The nasty rat, Templeton, acting out of purely selfish motives, obtains the necessary words Charlotte needs to weave into her web and later saves Charlotte's eggs, but he is still a rat. He was useful in the fight to save Wilbur, but his character remains the same. Being a hero is more than doing heroic things, it is doing them for the right reasons.

A FEW MORE THINGS TO PONDER . . .

Fern is desperate to save the little pig on the day he is born. She feels that it is terribly unfair to penalize him for being small, and her father listens to her argument for *justice* and changes his mind. Fern takes care of the piglet as a mother would a baby and, indeed, the *family* in this book includes parents, uncles, aunts, brother, sister, pig, geese, sheep, farmhand, and even a spider. In fact, Charlotte is very much like a mother to all the animals. Her love moves through every part of this story, and her *creativity* inspires the same in all of them. By the end, Fern and Wilbur teach us something about *growing up*; even the parents have learned and changed.

Reader's Guide

Heads Up *A little bit of extra help*

- Comment on the times when a character is a good friend, or a bad friend.
- Watch for each character's reaction to the idea of death.
- Point out how Wilbur shows his loneliness and fears.
- Look for changes that show Fern is growing up.

Dig Deeper *Some things to think about after you read*

1. Why did Fern's father think Wilbur was too much trouble? What is a runt?
2. Wilbur wasn't ready for the world outside the barn. Why is it sometimes scary to try new things?
3. Why did Fern hear the animals talk, while other people did not?
4. How did Charlotte first befriend Wilbur? What does that teach us about making friends?
5. Why did Templeton help Wilbur? Is the rat a hero?
6. How does Wilbur keep Charlotte's memory alive?

E. B. White must have loved animals. He wrote stories of a swan looking for his voice (*The Trumpet of the Swan*) and *Stuart Little*, the tale of a most adventurous mouse.

2

Hank the Cowdog
(series)

BY JOHN R. ERICKSON

Illustrated by Gerald L. Holmes

140 to 150 pages per book
1 to 2 hours of reading time
Ages 8 to 12

THEMES
*responsibility, heroism, freedom,
duty, courage, loyalty*

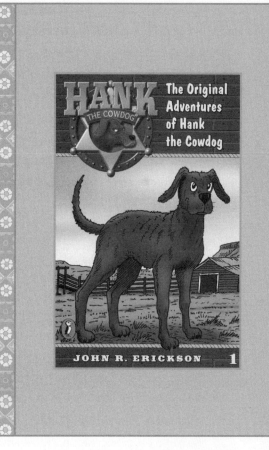

The Story

The Head of Ranch Security wakes up one morning to some bad news: there has been a murder committed right under his nose. Time to get to work and sniff out the culprit.

This particular security officer is Hank the Cowdog, and the victim is a chicken. Hank takes his job *very* seriously, but he's not very good at it, even though he sees himself as "a special kind of dog—strong, fearless, dedicated, and above all, smart."

When all his good intentions get him nowhere and Loper the cowboy accuses Hank of committing the chicken-house crimes, Hank decides to run away and become an outlaw. Yes, it is the free and easy wild life for Hank. He is tired of being unappreciated.

For a while he enjoys living in the coyote village, even though their meal choices are somewhat sickening, and he imagines he'll always feel like an outsider. Soon, though, Hank is asked to prove his loyalty to his new family by attacking his old friend at the ranch, and he is forced to make a decision between duty and his wilder side.

Whether he is saving the folks at the ranch from a blizzard, setting a trap for a thief, or just following his nose to some good eating, this cowdog's days are filled with adventure. Hank usually manages to find trouble, but his good heart always leads him back home.

A Page from *The Original Adventures of Hank the Cowdog*

I ran my eyes over the ranch I had loved and protected for so many years, waved farewell to Drover, and went on my way.

I wondered how Loper and Slim and Sally May would react when they figgered out that I had resigned and moved on. I had an idea they'd be sorry. They'd realize how they'd done me wrong and misjudged me and accused me of terrible things I didn't do. I mean, all I did was eat a dead chicken, and she wasn't a bit deader when I finished than when I started.

The Heart of the Book

Reading the thoughts of a cowdog who sees himself as the security chief of a ranch is a lot of fun. Hank's exploits are reminders of some interesting themes.

✿ *responsibility*
Most of the time Hank would rather be napping or rolling in the mud, but there is a vital job to be done and people to protect. Even though Hank's importance to the ranch is a little

overblown in his own mind, still he maintains that a dog in security work has to find his satisfaction "in knowing that you're doing the job right."

⚙ *heroism*

Hank tries not to take on more than he can handle, but when he has to, he will face up to danger to protect a friend or guard his territory. He may not always be the wisest dog, but most of the time he shows a great and gallant spirit.

⚙ *freedom*

Sometimes Hank's true animal nature gets the best of him and he experiments with the freedom of the wild. Living a life with no structure is not as much fun as it sounds, however, and he chooses the life he loves best—being the head dog at the ranch.

A FEW MORE THINGS TO PONDER . . .

When *duty* demands sacrifice, Hank finds the *courage* to answer the call. He sees himself as a dog with "a keen mind, a thick skin, and a peculiar devotion to duty," and though he sometimes leads where no one wants to follow, his *loyalty* is true.

📖 *Reader's Guide* _____

Heads Up   *A little bit of extra help*

* Find pictures of a skunk, a porcupine, a buzzard, and a coyote before you read, to help visualize what Hank is up against in some of these stories.
* You might want to start with the first book in the series, *The Original Adventures of Hank the Cowdog*.
* These stories are perfect for reading aloud with character voices.

Dig Deeper   *Some things to think about after you read*

1. How do you think Hank got his title, Head of Ranch Security?
2. Why does Hank like to keep Drover around?

3. How does Loper feel about Hank?
4. In *The Case of the Tricky Trap,* how does Hank find out that Eddy the Rac is a crook?
5. Why is Hank usually hungry for some real meat?
6. Hank certainly is up a tree in *The Fling.* How does he get there and why?
7. Hank gets into tons of trouble. How do we know that Sally May, Lope, Slim, and Alfred like him anyway?

- The buzzards and coyotes in these books are "scavengers." That means they prefer to eat dead, rotting animals. Yuck.
- There are almost fifty books in the Hank the Cowdog series.

3.

Little House on the Prairie
(series)

BY LAURA INGALLS WILDER

Illustrated by Garth Williams

335 pages per book
4 to 5 hours of reading time
Ages 8 to 12

THEMES
*work, self-sufficiency, family, nature,
history, constancy, adversity, environment*

The Story

Laura didn't always live in a little house on the prairie. Her first memories are of a warm and cozy home in the woods of Wisconsin, where she lived with Ma and Pa and her sisters, Mary and Carrie. Together they work and play, building a life far from any neighbors or family, but it is 1872 and civilization is creeping nearer to their cabin. Pa decides it is time to move west, and the Ingalls family goes from woods to prairie to town. There is the constant presence and sometimes threat of nature's wild beasts—bears, deer, and wolves—as well as bees and gigantic grasshoppers. The government runs the Ingallses off of Indian land, and sickness claims the life of a child and the eyesight of a sister. Life is hard but good, and Laura learns the precious lessons that equip her for a life on her own.

A Page from *Little House on the Prairie*

Laura was frightened. Jack had never growled at her before. Then she looked over her shoulder, where Jack was looking, and she saw two naked, wild men coming, one behind the other, on the Indian trail.

"Mary! Look!" she cried. Mary looked and saw them, too. They were tall, thin, fierce-looking men. Their skin was brownish-red. Their heads seemed to go up to a peak, and the peak was a tuft of hair that stood straight up and ended in feathers. Their eyes were black and still and glittering, like snake's eyes.

They came closer and closer. Then they went out of sight, on the other side of the house.

The Heart of the Book

Laura Ingalls Wilder describes a simpler time but not an easier life in the Little House series of books. There is a marked lack of self-pity or complaining from these characters, even though the lessons are sometimes tough ones.

✲ *work*

Morning comes early for this household, and the evening is filled with tasks to finish before the next day. Hard work is what has to be done if they are going to prosper or even survive.

⊛ self-sufficiency

By the time these girls leave home, they have watched their parents grow their own wheat and vegetables, make cheese from the milk of the cow they own, mold bullets, and even weave straw into next year's hats. They learn to take pride in this kind of independence.

⊛ family

Laura's world is her family. She is taught to respect her siblings and obey her parents, and in this safe setting she grows into a secure young woman.

⊛ nature

Laura notices the world around her: "But large stars hung from the sky, glittering so near that Laura felt she could almost touch them." She has the gift of awareness, and her descriptions of nature, brutal or beautiful, bring wonderful life to these pages.

⊛ history

These books are an easy-to-read glimpse into our history. The search for a better way to live is what propelled the pioneers forward, and along the way they invented, governed, negotiated, and passed wisdom from one generation to the next.

A FEW MORE THINGS TO PONDER . . .

Laura and her siblings count on the *constancy* of their parents, and thrive in this security, even as their life together changes. They face *adversity* and loss, but the fundamental *environment* of their lives is solid, and it is this they carry with them.

Reader's Guide

Heads Up   *A little bit of extra help*

- Keep a map handy while you read these books. It is very interesting to follow the Ingalls family across country as it is described in the story.

- Point out that the setting for these stories is after the Civil War.
- Notice the manner in which the author treats the Indian characters.
- Watch for the beautiful descriptions of seasons and natural beauty.

Dig Deeper *Some things to think about after you read*

1. Day to day, which animal is the most feared by Laura and her family?
2. What are some of the chores the children are given to do?
3. In each book, the family faces obstacles and tragedies that were common for pioneer families. What was their dilemma in *The Long Winter*?
4. How is Mary different from Laura? What are some things that make them jealous of each other?
5. What is the family's main entertainment?
6. Farm animals and wild animals are very important to the Ingallses' life. Name several ways they use animals.
7. Which time of year does Laura like the best? Why?

- Besides the Little House books, Garth Williams also illustrated *Charlotte's Web*, *The Rescuers*, *Stuart Little*, and *The Cricket in Times Square*.
- Summer pageants in modern-day De Smet, South Dakota, and Mansfield, Missouri, present reenactments of scenes from the Little House stories.

4.

Little Women

BY LOUISA MAY ALCOTT

500 pages, 12 to 15 hours of reading time
Ages 9 to 15

THEMES
*family, compassion, duty, work,
resourcefulness, adversity,
honesty, dignity*

The Story

The four March sisters live with their mother in a small New England town. The Civil War is raging and the family is limited by lack of money and troubled by the absence of their father, who has left to fight for the Union. The girls are bothered by the same issues that plague girls of every generation, but they survive their adventures and hardships because of the very close affection they feel for one another.

Meg is the oldest, sensible and sweet. Jo is a determined tomboy. Beth is shy and fragile and Amy is artistic and pretty. Each girl must learn her life lessons the hard way, and though the situations in which they find themselves are sometimes comical, these experiences help them begin to overcome their character flaws. The sisters are devoted to one another but they can sometimes be hurtful and cruel. Still, they struggle to mature and to develop good character. Their story also reveals a picture of the complex conflicts that can exist in women's lives. How will Jo come to terms with her aspirations as a writer? Is marriage right for every woman? It is within the safety of this nurturing home that the four sisters find the answers for themselves.

A Page from *Little Women*

"Are you sure she is safe?" whispered Jo, looking remorsefully at the golden head, which might have been swept away from her sight forever under the treacherous ice.

"Quite safe, dear. She is not hurt, and won't even take cold, I think, you were so sensible in covering and getting her home quickly," replied her mother cheerfully.

"Laurie did it all. I only let her go. Mother, if she *should* die, it would be my fault"; and Jo dropped down beside the bed, in a passion of penitent tears, telling all that had happened, bitterly condemning her hardness of heart, and sobbing out her gratitude for being spared the heavy punishment which might have come upon her.

"It's my dreadful temper! I try to cure it, I think I have, and then it breaks out worse than ever. Oh, Mother, what shall I do? What shall I do?" cried poor Jo, in despair.

"Watch and pray, dear, never get tired of trying, and never think it is impossible to conquer your fault," said Mrs. March, drawing the blowzy head to her shoulder and kissing the wet cheek so tenderly that Jo cried harder than ever.

The Heart of the Book

Louisa May Alcott ignores many of the restrictions that usually limited the works of writers of her era. She illustrates the complexities of life, showing both sides of marriage, materialism, romantic love, and emotions. Through the eyes and experiences of four very different girls and their mother, life is seen as full of difficult challenges, but ultimately deep and rich.

⊛ *family*

The women in the March household find the strength to face all kinds of troubles because they have the solid foundation of their family underneath them. When serious illness and even death visit them, they share the sorrow. Humiliation is not so tragic, fear is not so dark, because they have one another. Each finds her own happiness, and then multiplies it by giving it back to the others. Because they accept one another's faults as well as strengths, the family grows together instead of apart, even as they go their separate ways.

⊛ *compassion*

Marmee, mother to the four daughters, is a kind and uncomplaining woman, whose heart is tender toward the poor and hungry all around her. "And when they went away, leaving comfort behind, I think there were not in all the city four merrier people than the hungry little girls who gave away their breakfasts and contented themselves with bread and milk on Christmas morning." The girls can't help but be affected by her unselfish attitude as she encourages them to look beyond themselves.

⊛ *duty*

Much of the tension in this story comes from inside the minds of the girls themselves. Is their duty to the family or society, or should they commit themselves to becoming all that they want to be? The author uses each girl's personal journey to illustrate four different ways to answer this question.

A FEW MORE THINGS TO PONDER . . .

"Have regular hours for work and play; make each day both useful and pleasant, and prove that you understand the worth of time by employing it well. Then youth will be delightful, old age will bring few regrets, and life become a beautiful success, in spite of poverty." This good advice about *work, resourcefulness,* and how to combat the *adversity* of poverty comes from Marmee. The characters in the book also find that real *honesty* means being true to oneself, and that there is *dignity* in accepting small defeats and counting your blessings.

Reader's Guide

Heads Up *A little bit of extra help*

- This book takes place during wartime, and every family is living on less. Note the many times the March girls complain about their circumstances.
- Look for situations where they share troubles or worries.
- Think about why Alcott uses a few words from *Pilgrim's Progress* to begin her story.
- Point out the ways the family uses creativity to be resourceful.
- Notice how Marmee, the mother, teaches by example.

Dig Deeper *Some things to think about after you read*

1. A fun discussion could be had comparing girls today with the "little women" in the novel. Could four girls today be as close and sheltered as these sisters?
2. What do you think the author thought about formal education?
3. Are the girls encouraged to marry? Are they forced?
4. What are the conflicts each girl confronts within herself?
5. Mr. March is gone to war, but he is never far from the family's thoughts. How does he influence events from a distance?
6. Jo asks, "Wouldn't it be fun if all the castles in the air which we make could come true and we could live in them?" How close do the girls come to realizing their dreams?

Louisa May Alcott is pictured on the five-cent U.S. postage stamp issued in 1940 as part of the Famous American Authors series.

5.

Old Yeller

BY FRED GIPSON

167 pages, 3 to 4 hours of reading time
Ages 9 to 12

THEMES
*nature, coming of age, trust, courage,
responsibility, self-sufficiency*

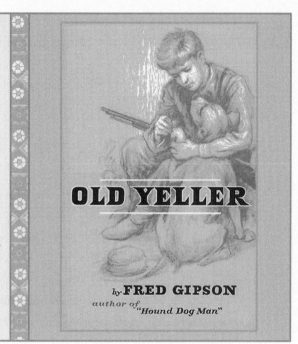

The Story

Fourteen-year-old Travis Coates is proud of his new role as the man of the house. Pa has gone off on a cattle drive, leaving Travis at home on the farm with his mother and little brother, and the boy is sure he is man enough for the job. Life on Birdsong Creek out in the Texas hill country isn't easy, but the family is accustomed to the hardship, and the little family settles in to try to manage without Pa for the months he is gone.

When a big ugly dog steals the last of the season's meat from its hook, Travis is furious, and even though his little brother, Arliss, pitches a fit and wants the dog as a pet, Travis starts trying to think of ways to get rid of him. Old Yeller wins his heart, though, when he saves Arliss from a mama bear. As Travis finds out over and over again, the old yellow dog with a chewed-off ear and a stub for a tail is the best friend he could ever hope to have.

Travis tells this story as a grown man looking back on this important time in his life. The dangers and adventures he experiences are all part of living as pioneers of a new territory in the 1860s. When Travis is faced with a heartbreaking decision after Old Yeller's fight with a rabid wolf, he learns for himself just how difficult it can be to take the step from being a child to being a man.

A Page from *Old Yeller*

Then, just as the bear went lunging up the creek bank toward little Arliss and her cub, a flash of yellow came streaking out of the brush.

It was that big yeller dog. He was roaring like a mad bull. He wasn't one-third as big and heavy as the she bear, but when he piled into her from one side, he rolled her clear off her feet. They went down in a wild, roaring tangle of twisting bodies and scrambling feet and slashing fangs.

As I raced past them, I saw the bear lunge up to stand on her hind feet like a man while she clawed at the body of the yeller dog hanging to her throat. I didn't wait to see more.

The Heart of the Book

This valuable book takes us back to a time in American history when families lived close to all of the danger and beauty of the land. Children grew into productive adults by facing the challenges of what was for them normal life.

✿ *nature*

The author paints a realistic view of life as it was for thousands of families during our country's early decades. This story shows us that while nature is, for the most part, a predictable partner with the homesteader, it can also be cruel and capricious. The soil, the rain, and the seasons provide food and shelter, but wild creatures, disease, and drought threaten a family's very existence.

✺ coming of age

"I guessed that I could handle things while Papa was gone just about as good as he could." Because his father has taught him many useful skills, Travis imagines at the beginning of the story that he is "pretty near a grown man." He does prove himself to be very capable at protecting his family and doing the hard work on the farm, but it is learning to accept the bad with the good and moving on with an optimistic outlook that set him on the path to manhood.

✺ trust

To say the least, Travis is wary of the "thieving rascal" dog that shows up at the farm. He admits that the dog is smart, but he still doesn't want him around. Over time, the loyalty and protectiveness that Old Yeller shows toward Travis and his family turn the boy's heart, and they forge a bond. This is a reminder of the trust that was essential in the homesteader's world, where family members relied on one another and neighbor helped neighbor.

A FEW MORE THINGS TO PONDER . . .

It takes bravery to risk making a living out in the Texas hill country, and Travis has obviously seen this modeled in his parents, but he learns a different kind of *courage* by the end of the story. The *responsibility* he takes on as a natural part of his life builds his pride and confidence, as does the *self-sufficiency* the Coates family has developed by growing and hunting everything they need for food and shelter.

Reader's Guide

Heads Up *A little bit of extra help*

- Point out how busy a typical farm day was for the Coates family.
- Look for ways we see death as part of life all through the story.
- Some things never change. Note how the Coates family is like a modern family, especially in relationships.
- Notice how the author warns us that something exciting is about to happen.

Dig Deeper *Some things to think about after you read*

1. How does Travis try to show his maturity as his father is preparing to leave on the cattle drive?
2. Why did Travis suddenly feel affection for Old Yeller?
3. What is hydrophobia?
4. Are the female characters strong people in this story?
5. There is one thing the homesteaders can't grow or hunt, and it is what Pa is after when he goes on the cattle drive. What is it?
6. How does Travis find out how dear his little brother really is to him?
7. How does Travis recover from feeling "dead and empty" over losing Old Yeller?

- *Old Yeller* was made into a popular Walt Disney movie in 1957. The author, Fred Gipson, cowrote the screenplay.
- Other books about animals include *Gentle Ben, Sounder, Island of the Blue Dolphins, The Yearling,* and *Call of the Wild.*

6.

The People Could Fly

BY VIRGINIA HAMILTON

Illustrated by Leo and Diane Dillon

192 pages, 24 folktales, 5 to 15 minutes of
reading time for each folktale
Ages 5 to 9

THEMES
*fear, resourcefulness, intelligence, nature,
adversity, independence*

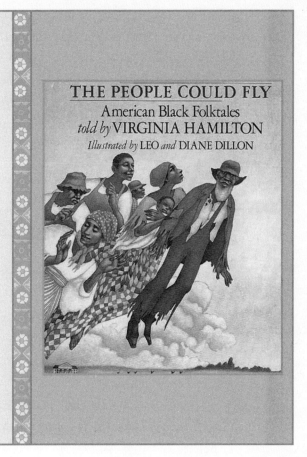

THE PEOPLE COULD FLY
American Black Folktales
told by VIRGINIA HAMILTON
Illustrated by LEO *and* DIANE DILLON

The Story

Sometimes in short, entertaining episodes and other times in factual accounts of danger and flight, the characters in *The People Could Fly* come to life. What a trick Wiley plays on the Hairy Man, proving that sometimes the weak do indeed overcome the strong. Is Nehemiah smart enough to outwit the owner of the plantation and gain his freedom? Bruh Fox sure knows how to make good use of Tar Baby, but Bruh Fox fools him in the end, and Jake is glad to be on a horse called Fastest when he has to outrace the pumpkin vine. Wolf can't stop himself from insulting the birds that have loaned him some feathers so he can fly. One by one they take their feathers back. It seems Wolf just never learns.

In this collection, American black folktales are told in a readable but colloquial voice that, as the author says, "reflects the expressiveness of the original slave teller." The storyteller shows the reader who's the *real* king of the forest, shares the very scary outcome of any encounter with the devil, and tells the first-person slave stories of freedom. The collection is a fascinating glimpse into the memory of the ancestors of a people.

A Page from *The People Could Fly*

Bruh Rabbit just say, "Mebbe you right, Bruh Gator. We on the land seein a lot a trouble."

"What Trouble is?" asked Bruh Gator.

Bruh Rabbit can't believe it. "You sayin you never know trouble yet?"

"Never know nothin about him," Bruh Gator say. "How just do Trouble look? How him stand?"

It then Bruh Rabbit catch on. He know a way to shut he Gator mouth about them is livin on land. He show Bruh Gator he place and have fun with him besides.

"Don't know can tell you how Trouble lookin, Bruh Gator, nor how he standin. But maybe I can show you him, you get on come tomorra," Bruh Rabbit say.

The Heart of the Book

Some of these tales are told just for entertainment, but there are lessons in many of them.

✦ *fear*

He Lion can roar all he likes but he's no match for the man and his gun. He learns it is better to be realistic in his boasting. On the other hand, many characters in these stories show a healthy fear but outwit the more powerful in the end.

✦ *resourcefulness*

Little John uses a horsehide and even his grandmother to defeat the evil intentions of Big John. The slave resorts to riddles to gain his freedom. These tales always celebrate ingenuity.

✦ *intelligence*

It is fun to watch these characters employ their brains to outsmart one another. A universal theme of folktales is the idea that a well-planned scheme or a cleverly turned question will defeat the big-mouth every time.

✦ *nature*

People who were trying to survive in a strange new land passed along these stories. Assigning personality traits to animals gave them a safe way to express their understanding of the world around them.

A FEW MORE THINGS TO PONDER . . .

Though slaves faced the cruelest *adversity* and were forced into complete subservience in order to survive, these tales reflect the beautiful *independence* of the human spirit as it imagines and pursues freedom.

Reader's Guide

Heads Up   *A little bit of extra help*

- Note that the stories don't always have a happy ending.
- Watch for the theme of freedom, both in the first-person stories and the fanciful tales.
- Imagine the settings in which these folktales were passed along.

Dig Deeper   *Some things to think about after you read*

1. In "He Lion, Bruh Bear, and Bruh Rabbit" the nine-year-old boy and the ninety-year-old man have names. What are they?
2. In which stories do the characters use wordplay to outwit an enemy?
3. What clever trick is used in "How Nehemiah Got Free"?
4. Which animals are smart?
5. How does Trouble look when Bruh Gator meets him?
6. Is the story *The People Could Fly* fact or fantasy?
7. How might these stories have helped slaves to survive?

Many of these stories were first told in the Gullah language. "Gullah" comes from the word "Angola," a country in Africa. Gullah slaves lived mainly on islands off the coast of South Carolina.

7.

Where the Red Fern Grows

BY WILSON RAWLS

215 pages, 3 to 4 hours of reading time
Ages 9 to 12

THEMES
*determination, loyalty, responsibility,
obedience, self-esteem, growing up, nature*

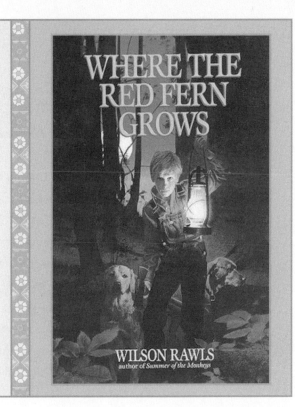

The Story

Billy lies in his bed at night and listens longingly to the sounds of hunters and their hounds climbing hills and crossing rivers in pursuit of that most elusive forest animal, the raccoon. At ten, all Billy wants in the world is to hunt coons with a couple of hound dogs he can call his own. His family works a farm in the hills of the Ozarks, and they certainly cannot afford to buy him any dogs, but Billy has an idea. He will save enough money to buy them himself. For two years he provides bait to the men who fish the river, traps animals for the furs, and picks berries to sell in his grandfather's store. Finally he collects enough cash and buys two redbone hound pups.

Billy trains his dogs to hunt coons, and their nighttime adventures become the most important thing in his life. Over and over the dogs prove themselves as loyal companions and the best hunters in the Ozarks. Billy experiences the miracles of nature and answered prayer, but it is his eventual confrontation with tragedy that helps to turn him into a man.

A Page from *Where the Red Fern Grows*

Across the river and from far back in the rugged mountains I heard the baying of a hound. I wondered if it was the same one I had heard from my window on those nights so long ago.

Although my eyes were seeing the wonders of the night, my ears were ever alert, listening for the sound of my hounds telling me they had found a trail.

I was expecting one of them to bawl, but when it came it startled me. The deep tones of Old Dan's voice jarred the silence around me. I dropped my ax and almost dropped my lantern. A strange feeling came over me. I took a deep breath and threw back my head to give the call of the hunter, but something went wrong. My throat felt like it had been tied in a knot. I swallowed a couple of times and the knot disappeared.

As loud as I could, I whooped, "Who-e-e-e. Get him, Dan. Get him."

The Heart of the Book

Billy's dedication to his dogs, Big Dan and Little Ann, and to hunting proves to be good for the family and for him, but the lessons learned in this story are difficult ones. For a poor family in the Ozarks, life is full of hard work and worry. Billy loves the beautiful woods and the chase of the hounds, but he finds it is a dangerous world as well.

✸ *determination*
Billy is very much like his hound dogs. When he resolves to do something, he shows amazing willpower in accomplishing the task. Many of his challenges are almost impossi-

ble, and some are life-and-death struggles. Determination is "a good thing for a man to have," as Grandpa says. "It goes a long way in his life." It is what makes Billy's dream of owning hound dogs come true, assures the successful hunt, and many times saves the lives of his dogs.

⚙ *loyalty*

From the beginning, Billy is devoted to his pups. The very first night he owns them, he stays up all night in a cave to protect them from a mountain lion. He is "ready to die" for his dogs. He proves his love for them over and over when they are in trouble. They repay him with complete devotion. The story shows that there is a kind of loyalty that the dogs have for one another, too, even if their lives are at stake.

⚙ *responsibility*

Billy's transition from a boy to a man begins with his realization that he can buy the pups if he works hard and saves the money for the purchase. He decides to stop asking his parents for the money and to take on the challenge himself. With this responsibility comes much sacrifice, but much larger rewards. Not only does Billy learn the joy of accomplishment, he also sees firsthand how hard work can improve the welfare of his family.

⚙ *obedience*

The respect that these family members have for one another is clear. Billy loves and honors his parents, but as he is turning from childhood he begins to make his own decisions and struggles with the restrictions his mother wants to put on him. Billy is never sneaky but, just as his hounds do not always obey him if their nature dictates otherwise, Billy learns to set some of his own rules as he becomes a man.

A FEW MORE THINGS TO PONDER . . .

Billy's *self-esteem* grows in a natural and healthy way as he is put to the test on the hunt and with people. His *growing-up* process takes place not only out in the woods, confronting danger with his hounds, but also in his conflicts with the ugly side of human character. Both the harshness and grandeur of *nature* are explored, with beautiful depictions of bright moonlit nights, crushing blizzards, and swaying sycamore branches.

Heads Up *A little bit of extra help*

- Look for situations where Billy must set a goal.
- This family lives off the land, by farming, hunting, and trapping, and many of the scenes involve the death of animals.
- Watch for any hints early in the book of the way the story will end.
- Notice the effect Billy's faith in God has on his actions.
- Point out the indications that this family has very little material wealth.

Dig Deeper *Some things to think about after you read*

1. Why did Billy's mother own the land they lived on?
2. Billy didn't tell his family that he was saving money. Why?
3. Billy's description of his experiences in town upset his mother. How did this make her more determined about the future?
4. Little Ann and Old Dan are bonded to each other in some unusual ways. Describe how this is shown in the story.
5. Billy tells this story as an adult. Do you think he is happy he had the two hounds as a child?
6. What is the legend of the red fern? How does the red fern help Billy begin to heal after his dogs die?

- Wilson Rawls also wrote *Summer of the Monkeys,* the story of a boy who sets out to capture monkeys who escaped from the circus.
- The ancestors of the redbone hound were foxhounds. Redbones are well known for their agility, and for their ability in trailing not only "Mr. Ringtail" but also many other kinds of wild game.

8.

Winnie-the-Pooh (series)

BY A. A. MILNE

Illustrated by Ernest H. Shepard

160 pages per book
2 to 3 hours of reading time
Ages 5 to 9

THEMES
*friendship, encouragement, generosity,
imagination, individuality*

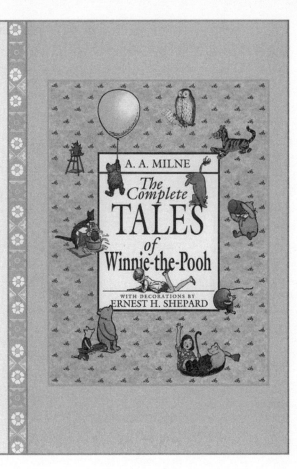

The Story

How nice it must be for Christopher Robin to have so many very good friends. Of course, they aren't perfect, but he loves them all and they love him. Winnie-the-Pooh is always close by, and though Pooh believes he is a "Bear with Very Little Brain," he can often be quite sensible, even if he lapses into whimsy once in a while. There is shy little Piglet, gloomy Eeyore, and the very verbal Owl. There is Rabbit and his relations, rambunctious Tigger, sweet Roo, and his mother, Kanga. These friends live a simple and happy life in and around the Hundred Acre Wood but that doesn't mean that excitement can't be found. What if a bear needs the honey in the top of the tree? He can always float up with a balloon. What if a donkey loses his tail? It might be stuck on Owl's front door. And besides all of those important things to do, it is always a good thing to look out for Heffalumps and Woozles, find a yummy breakfast of marmalade and honeycomb, or just go humming along and visit with the best friends in the world.

A Page from *Winnie-the-Pooh*

The Piglet was sitting on the ground at the door of his house blowing happily at a dandelion, and wondering whether it would be this year, next year, sometime or never. He had just discovered that it would be never, and was trying to remember what *"it"* was, and hoping it wasn't anything nice, when Pooh came up.

"Oh! Piglet," said Pooh excitedly, "we're going on an Expotition, all of us, with things to eat. To discover something."

"To discover what?" said Piglet anxiously.

"Oh! Just something."

"Nothing fierce?"

"Christopher Robin didn't say anything about fierce. He just said it had an 'x'."

"It isn't their necks I mind," said Piglet earnestly. "It's their teeth. But if Christopher Robin is coming I don't mind anything."

The Heart of the Book

Christopher Robin and his friends remind us of people we know: Owls who use big words and seem to know everything, busy Rabbits who are orderly and always ready with a plan. Pooh is very much like any other lovable friend who hums absentmindedly and has a huge heart.

✺ *friendship*

These companions sometimes get their feelings hurt, often do the wrong thing while trying to decide the best thing, but always have the right intentions.

✺ *encouragement*

Rabbit knows Piglet is small but useful and that Pooh is large but important. By pointing out each other's strengths, even while acknowledging the not-so-strong parts, the characters help one another.

✺ *generosity*

Many of the adventures in these books happen because the friends decide to give someone a special something. Piglet and Pooh want Eeyore to have a house and Christopher Robin plans a party for Pooh. The stories are filled with simple acts of generosity.

A FEW MORE THINGS TO PONDER . . .
The life of a child should be filled with opportunities for *imagination* to flourish. Christopher Robin's animal toys are real to him, each with its own unique personality. *Winnie-the-Pooh* encourages us to celebrate the *individuality* that is a part of every person.

📖 *Reader's Guide* _____

Heads Up   *A little bit of extra help*

- Look for ways that the characters show friendship.
- Point out how Pooh, Piglet, Owl, and Eeyore display generosity.
- Take a look at the map of the story's setting at the front of the book.

Dig Deeper   *Some things to talk about after you read*

1. Do you know anyone like Eeyore or any of the other characters?
2. Which character is a little forgetful? Which one is talkative?

3. Encourage a discussion about make-believe friends.
4. How does Piglet encourage Pooh?
5. In which stories do Eeyore's friends show him kindness?
6. What kinds of trouble does Pooh get in?

- *Winnie-the-Pooh* has been translated into thirty-three languages. The Latin translation, *Winnie ille Pu,* was the first foreign language book to make the *New York Times* bestseller list.
- Ernest Shepard, the artist who created the drawings of the characters in *Winnie-the-Pooh,* also illustrated many other books, including Kenneth Grahame's *The Wind in the Willows.*

Books to Read to and

with Young Children

9.

Goodnight Moon

BY MARGARET WISE BROWN

Illustrated by Clement Hurd

32 pages, 5 to 10 minutes of reading time
Infants to age 5

THEMES
*bedtime, comfort, growing up,
constancy, individuality*

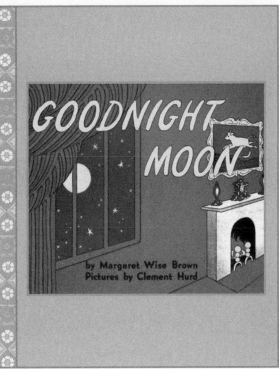

The Story

A little bunny is all tucked in and ready for bed in a big green room with a fireplace and the stars shining outside the window. It is time to go to sleep, but first he must say good night to every single thing in the room. As the moon rises across the sky, the room gets darker and the bunny, warm and safe, falls asleep.

The Heart of the Book

For over fifty years, millions of readers have read their children to sleep with *Goodnight Moon*. This little book holds some special gifts for little ones.

bedtime

It is easier to settle down and go to sleep when a little bunny shows you how. Sometimes it also helps to say good night to the familiar things a child keeps close by.

comfort

The repetition and rhyme in Brown's story are just part of the comforting feeling of *Goodnight Moon*. The balanced colors and shapes, the fireplace, the "quiet old lady"—all of these things make a child feel safe.

growing up

Learning to separate from a parent and fall asleep alone is a big step for a child. The rituals and rhythms encouraged in this little book make this a pleasurable time.

A FEW MORE THINGS TO PONDER . . .

The light grows dimmer and the activity stops, but there is a secure feeling of *constancy* in the sameness of the room as the minutes pass. Young children begin to experience their own *individuality* as they see themselves as separate from the other things in the green room.

Reader's Guide

Heads Up   A little bit of extra help

- The illustrator's use of color and shapes creates a comforting, childlike atmosphere.
- The shift from color to black-and-white focuses a child's attention.

Dig Deeper   Some things to think about after you read

1. What are some of the nice things the bunny has in his room?
2. The old lady quietly leaves the room. Who takes her place in the rocking chair?
3. What are some things in your room that you would like to say good night to?

The frame on the left wall of the "great green room" holds a picture from another famous Margaret Wise Brown book: *The Runaway Bunny*.

10

Babar (series)

WRITTEN AND ILLUSTRATED BY JEAN DE BRUNHOFF AND LAURENT DE BRUNHOFF

40 to 50 pages each
15 to 20 minutes of reading time
Ages 3 to 7

THEMES
*compassion, hope, courage,
comfort, individuality*

The Story

Babar is a young elephant who is loved and happy in the great forest. Suddenly a hunter kills his mother and Babar must run away to escape the hunter's trap. He finds himself in a big city, where a kind old lady helps him become sophisticated and elegant, buying him new clothes and a fine education. Soon he goes back to the forest to be crowned King of the Elephants. One excitement follows another as Babar and his queen, Celeste, are trapped by a circus troupe, outsmart Rataxes and the rhinos, and build a splendid city. Always rising to the challenge, Babar proves himself a wise and noble king and a friend to every child who meets him through these stories.

The Heart of the Book

Babar is a sensible and loving hero. By the end of each book, children feel reassured, having seen their friend Babar find a terrific solution to tough problems once again.

⚙ *compassion*
Babar shows great gentleness to his family and friends. He is compassionate when Cornelius is injured in a fire, and shows love for Madame all through the stories.

⚙ *hope*
"Remember that in this life we must never lose heart." That is Madame's reminder to Babar at the end of *Babar the King*. Bad things happen sometimes, but we must always hope for the best.

⚙ *courage*
From the beginning, Babar has the strength to face big obstacles. As an orphan, he must overcome his sadness and make his way in the big city. As he gets older, he leads in battles and escapes from captivity. This brave elephant never runs from a challenge.

A FEW MORE THINGS TO PONDER . . .

There are many cozy moments of *comfort* in the Babar books. Madame takes care of Babar in the big city, and Celeste comforts her baby, Flora. The *individuality* of each character is encouraged and celebrated in these stories.

Reader's Guide

Heads Up *A little bit of extra help*

- Be aware that there are situations in the Babar stories that might be troubling for some children: a mother elephant is killed, there are some intense pictures of a nightmare, and an elephant dies after eating a poisonous mushroom.
- De Brunhoff's gentle illustrations are filled with detail. Looking closely, little eyes will find such delights as a man diving off a pier in the distance and houses hanging from trees in Monkeyville.

Dig Deeper *Some things to think about after you read*

1. What was the scariest moment in the story? What was the funniest?
2. Who is Babar's best friend?
3. What are the names of Babar's children?
4. Do you think Babar is a good king? Why?

- Jean de Brunhoff was a painter in France. He wrote and illustrated the original Babar stories after hearing his wife tell the story of a little elephant to their sons.
- After his father died, Laurent de Brunhoff began creating his own Babar books.

11.

Carlo Likes Reading

BY JESSICA SPANYOL

32 pages, 15 to 20 minutes of reading time
Ages 2 to 6

THEMES
education, helpfulness, comfort, friendship

The Story

Carlo is one lucky giraffe. He loves to read, and everything in his world is nicely labeled for him. He can learn to spell and recognize words everywhere he goes, from the garage to the market to the duck pond, and his friends and family are all part of the fun.

A Page from *Carlo Likes Reading*

Carlo reads to some ducks.
Carlo reads at the market.
Carlo likes reading very much.

The Heart of the Book

Carlo is happiest when he is reading. Each page of this book is an invitation to the joy of learning new things.

⚙ *education*
The bright drawings and easy-to-read words make learning fun for the new reader, and Carlo's attitude toward reading is infectious.

⚙ *helpfulness*
This generous giraffe takes time to read to babies and his cat—even to the ducks.

⚙ *comfort*
The mommy giraffe nuzzles little Carlo while she reads a book to him, and the cozy environment seems more safe and secure because each object is labeled in such a clean, clear way.

A FEW MORE THINGS TO PONDER . . .
The reader sees *friendship* between Carlo and the other characters in the story, and the presence of the common objects lends warm familiarity.

Heads Up *A little bit of extra help*

- Look forward to the thrill of watching the little reader make the connection between objects and words, and between sounds and letters.
- It might be fun to label a few things around the house or yard to make this time together even more effective.

Dig Deeper *Some things to think about after you read*

1. Carlo's dad has four signs on him that say the same thing. What is the word on the signs?
2. What does Carlo read with his friend Nevil?
3. What else does Carlo love to do besides read?

Jessica Spanyol wrote more about this lovable giraffe in *Carlo Likes Counting* and *Carlo Likes Colors*.

12

Clifford, the Big Red Dog

(series)

WRITTEN AND ILLUSTRATED BY NORMAN BRIDWELL

32 pages each
3 to 5 minutes of reading time
Ages 3 to 6

THEMES
*respect, courtesy, heroism, responsibility,
fairness, cooperation*

The Story

When Clifford was born, he wasn't big at all. In fact, he was the runt of the litter, but little Emily Elizabeth loved him so much that he grew, and grew some more. Soon he was bigger than a house. Emily has to bathe him in the swimming pool. His howling can break the windows in the neighborhood. He's so big that Emily gives him his treats from a second-story window. He always tries to do the right thing but he "has *some* bad habits,"

Emily admits, like catching cars in his mouth and digging up trees. He's red and warm and a little goofy, and all children wish they had Clifford for a pet.

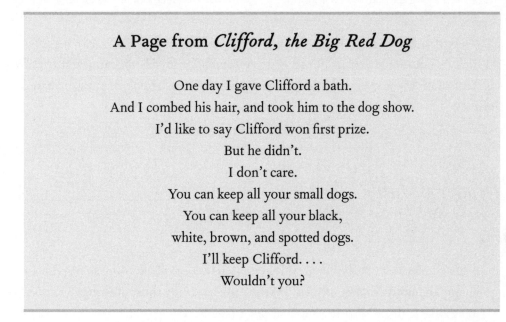

A Page from *Clifford, the Big Red Dog*

One day I gave Clifford a bath.
And I combed his hair, and took him to the dog show.
I'd like to say Clifford won first prize.
But he didn't.
I don't care.
You can keep all your small dogs.
You can keep all your black,
white, brown, and spotted dogs.
I'll keep Clifford. . . .
Wouldn't you?

The Heart of the Book

It is big fun having Clifford for a pet, but it can make for big problems, too. Silly solutions and outrageous results hide a few subtle lessons.

✪ *respect*
In spite of his mistakes, Emily loves Clifford just the way he is. Accepting other people's differences and treating them with kindness is the first step in learning how to respect others.

✪ *courtesy*
Clifford's Manners, another book in the series, is all about learning to be polite. Kids find out that using common courtesy with their friends and family makes every activity easier.

⊛ *heroism*

"Good old Clifford saved the day." Clifford uses his size to help people out of jams, proving that even a dog can be a hero when he looks out for the needs of those around him.

A FEW MORE THINGS TO PONDER . . .

With Emily's encouragement, Clifford takes *responsibility* for his mistakes and tries to fix them. The solutions the characters find for the situations in each book emphasize *fairness* and *cooperation*.

Reader's Guide

Heads Up   *A little bit of extra help*

- Bridwell uses a dry storytelling style and often uses his illustrations to provide the humor and heart of these stories. Take the time to enjoy these drawings and point out things like Clifford's expressions and other details.
- It's a good idea to start enjoying this series with the first book, *Clifford, the Big Red Dog.*

Dig Deeper   *Some things to think about after you read*

1. Why did Clifford grow so big?
2. How did Emily's family get him out of the backyard when they moved to the country?
3. In *Clifford and the Big Parade*, how does Clifford save the day?
4. What is hidden in Clifford's birthday cake in *Clifford's Birthday Party*?

There are more than forty books so far in the Clifford series.

13.

Corduroy

WRITTEN AND
ILLUSTRATED BY
DON FREEMAN

32 pages, 5 to 10 minutes of reading time
Ages 3 to 7

THEMES
*inclusion, hope, individuality, loneliness,
resourcefulness, flaws, love, fear*

The Story

Corduroy the teddy bear was so sad, sitting on the department-store shelf waiting for someone to love him and take him home. When he is passed over by a little girl's mother because he is missing a button, he is dismayed but decides to do something about it. Late that night, Corduroy goes looking for his lost button but finds himself in a bit of trouble instead, and soon he is back on the shelf. He has had quite an adventure going up a "mountain" and visiting a "palace," but when the little girl appears again in the toy department, he knows that a home is what he wants most of all.

A Page from *Corduroy*

All at once he saw something small and round.

"Why, here's my button!" he cried. And he tried to pick it up. But, like all the other buttons on the mattress, it was tied down tight.

He yanked and pulled with both paws until POP! Off came the button—and off the mattress Corduroy toppled, *bang* into a tall floor lamp. Over it fell with a crash!

The Heart of the Book

Corduroy's childlike ways and courageous attitude make him an endearing, inspirational character.

✪ *inclusion*
What the teddy bear longs for most of all is a place to belong. He finds it at last in the girl's home.

✪ *hope*
Even though he has been sitting in the department store a long time, Corduroy does not lose hope. Every day he waits for the right person to pick him up.

✪ *individuality*
The little girl is drawn to Corduroy in particular. "Look! There's the very bear I've always wanted."

✪ *loneliness*
Both the little girl and Corduroy are in need of friendship, and they express it in a simple, vulnerable way.

A FEW MORE THINGS TO PONDER . . .

Corduroy doesn't just sit on the shelf. He uses great *resourcefulness* to try to remedy the situation. The mother sees the missing button as a *flaw,* but the little girl's *love* is unconditional, and that love removes Corduroy's *fear* of being alone.

Reader's Guide

Heads Up *A little bit of extra help*

- Some children like to have their own teddy bear with them when they read this classic.
- *Corduroy* is a very nice choice for a bedtime story.

Dig Deeper *Some things to think about after you read*

1. Why was Corduroy sad?
2. Why did he want to find his button? Did he find it?
3. How do you suppose the night watchman thought Corduroy got upstairs?
4. What is your favorite thing about the little girl's room?

- First available for sale in 1902, teddy bears are still the most popular stuffed animal sold today.
- Winnie-the-Pooh and Paddington Bear are two other famous fictional teddy bears.

14.

Frances the Badger
(series)

BY RUSSELL HOBAN

*Illustrated by Garth Williams
and Lillian Hoban*

32 pages each
15 to 20 minutes of reading time
Ages 4 to 6

THEMES
*comfort, cooperation, generosity,
bedtime, obedience, friendship*

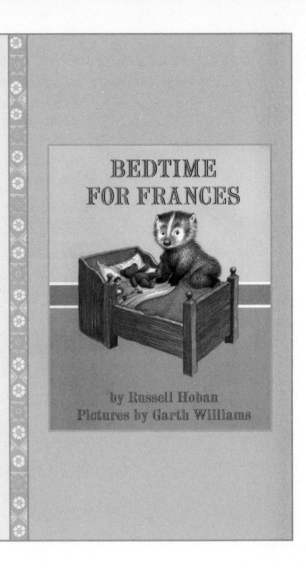

The Story

Frances knows it is her bedtime because the clock says so. Her mother says so. Her father says so. But it is not so easy for little badgers to go to sleep, even after a glass of milk and extra kisses. Her teddy bear keeps her company, but still she thinks of lots of reasons to get out of bed just one more time.

On another day, Frances becomes frustrated with her choice of playmates, but in the end figures out the best way to have best friends. In yet another lesson for the little badger, she discovers the unhappy side of being a picky eater. Cuddly and cute, Frances makes her way through all of the normal problems of childhood.

A Page from *Bedtime for Frances*

She was sure she could see a tiger.
She went to tell Mother and Father.
"There is a tiger in my room," said Frances.
"Did he bite you?" said Father.
"No," said Frances.
"Did he scratch you?" said Mother.
"No," said Frances.
"Then he is a friendly tiger," said Father.

The Heart of the Book

Children have no trouble relating to Frances the badger, because she behaves like a typical four- or five-year-old. The gentle circumstances in which she learns her lessons are soothing to the little reader.

✿ comfort

The reader sees Frances confront all the same distractions and fears that most children face at bedtime, or watches as she feels left out because of a new baby in the house. It is comforting to discover that everything turns out just fine.

✿ cooperation

Frances and her pals learn that working together in friendship and in the family is the best way to be happy.

✦ *generosity*

When it is time to give her sister a birthday present, Frances finds that her best intentions compete with her own wants. Children learn that generosity is a good thing.

A FEW MORE THINGS TO PONDER . . .

Frances learns all about the rules regarding *bedtime*. Good lessons about *obedience* and *friendship* are taught in funny and memorable ways.

📖 Reader's Guide

Heads Up   *A little bit of extra help*

- Frances loves to express her feelings with songs. Try making up melodies to sing her thoughts to your young reader.
- Explain what a badger is to your child.

Dig Deeper   *Some things to think about after you read*

1. What kind of an animal is Frances?
2. Frances has a hard time falling asleep in *Bedtime for Frances*. Why?
3. Who are Frances's friends in *Best Friends for Frances*? What kinds of things do they do together?
4. Frances has a little sister. What is her name? What does Frances like about having a sister? What does she not like?

The six titles in the Frances series are: *Bedtime for Frances. A Baby Sister for Frances, Bread and Jam for Frances, A Birthday for Frances, Best Friends for Frances, A Bargain for Frances*

15.

Hop on Pop

**WRITTEN AND
ILLUSTRATED BY
DR. SEUSS**

64 pages, 10 minutes of reading time
Ages 4 to 7

THEMES
imagination, growing up, family, creativity

HOP
ON
POP

By Dr. Seuss

The SIMPLEST SEUSS
for YOUNGEST USE

The Story

Odd, friendly characters skip from page to page in *Hop on Pop*. They practice simple words as they balance precariously on a wall or fall asleep with their glasses on. These funny animals recite rhymes as they catapult Mr. Brown into the air or engage in one of their most outrageous habits—playing all day and fighting all night.

A Page from *Hop on Pop*

Pup is down.
Where is Brown?
WHERE IS BROWN?
THERE IS BROWN!
Mr. Brown is out of town.

The Heart of the Book

Besides introducing words in a fun way to the reader, there are some other important ideas.

⚙ *imagination*
"Fish in a tree? How can that be?" It's fun to learn to read with some of these unlikely pairings.

⚙ *growing up*
Little brothers read little words and fathers read big words, and the reader is in-between. Learning is part of growing up.

⚙ *family*
Father, Mother, sister, brother, and other brother—all together they make a family, with everyone fitting in nicely. Just don't hop on Pop.

A FEW MORE THINGS TO PONDER . . .
By turning the world upside down and then putting it right again, Dr. Seuss keeps a child laughing and learning, and encourages *creativity*.

Reader's Guide

Heads Up   *A little bit of extra help*

- The action in *Hop on Pop* is sometimes hilariously unpredictable, but this is not confusing to a new reader. Note how the illustrations help a child trace each word to its meaning.
- Some children like to act out the events in *Hop on Pop*.

Dig Deeper   *Some things to think about after you read*

1. What are three silly things that Pat does?
2. Why did the little girl say good-bye to the singing Thing?
3. Find the word "fall" in the book.
4. Find the word "hill."

- Theodor Geisel (Dr. Seuss) won the Pulitzer Prize and three Academy Awards. He was the author and illustrator of forty-four children's books, and died in 1991. He continues to be one of the best-selling authors of children's books in the world.
- Some other Dr. Seuss favorites are: *The Cat in the Hat, Horton Hatches the Egg, and The 500 Hats of Bartholomew Cubbins.*

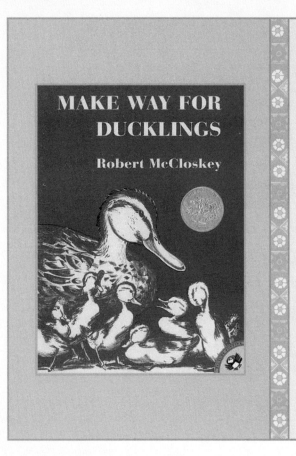

16

Make Way for Ducklings

WRITTEN AND
ILLUSTRATED BY
ROBERT MCCLOSKEY

32 pages, 10 to 15 minutes of reading time
Ages 4 to 8

THEMES
helpfulness, obedience, courtesy,
nature, comfort

The Story

Mr. and Mrs. Mallard are in a hurry to find a new home. Soon they will have a family of ducklings to take care of and they must find a safe spot away from foxes and turtles. They finally choose an island in the middle of the Charles River in Boston, but when the babies are hatched, how will they ever make it through the busy traffic of the city to their final home in the Public Garden? Leave it to their policeman friend, Michael, to lend a helping hand. Soon Mrs. Mallard and her eight ducklings are safe and settled for good in the garden pond.

The cars kept speeding by and honking, and Mrs. Mallard and the ducklings kept right on quack-quack-quacking.

They made such a noise that Michael came running, waving his arms and blowing his whistle.

The Heart of the Book

This sweet little story encourages first steps in important directions.

⚙ *helpfulness*

Without Michael's kind actions, the Mallard family would have had a hard time getting through the city streets.

⚙ *obedience*

It was very important that the ducklings learn how to obey their mother in order to be kept safe from harm and not get lost.

⚙ *courtesy*

"'Good morning,' quacked Mr. Mallard, being polite." Manners are always a good idea, even with a "strange, enormous bird."

A FEW MORE THINGS TO PONDER . . .

The reader learns a little about **nature** as the Mallard parents shed their feathers and wait for their eggs to hatch. The ducklings take **comfort** in their mother's care for them.

Reader's Guide

Heads Up   *A little bit of extra help*

- A fun thing to mention before reading the book is that Robert McCloskey was inspired to write *Make Way for Ducklings* after noticing a duck family in Boston's Public Garden.
- Notice how interesting the illustrations are, even though they are done in only one color.

Dig Deeper   *Some things to think about after you read*

1. Why couldn't Mr. and Mrs. Mallard fly for a little while?
2. What are some reasons it was good for the ducklings to learn to obey their mother?
3. How did Michael show kindness to the Mallard family?

After the publication of the book in 1941, the author of *Make Way for Ducklings* received reports every week about duck families sighted on city streets.

17.

Mother Goose Rhymes

300 to 400 short verses

Ages 1 to 5

THEMES

nature, bedtime, prudence, work, love

The Story

Humpty Dumpty, Little Miss Muffett, Ladybird, Polly, Jack, and Mary with her lamb have been dear friends of children for over two centuries. "This little pig" jumps across little toes, the baker teaches tiny hands to "pat-a-cake," and the "itsy bitsy spider" coaxes fingers up the waterspout. The Mother Goose characters never grow old and never cease to fascinate babies and toddlers.

The Heart of the Book

Mother Goose Rhymes are fun to hear because of their rhythm and rhyme, but there are also some important principles to learn.

⚙ *nature*

Little reminders and old farmers' sayings pop up in these pages: "If chickens roll in the sand, rain is sure to be at hand."

⚙ *bedtime*

Lots of little ones have been rocked to sleep with these timeworn verses, like "Rock-a-bye Baby" and "Sleep, Baby, Sleep."

⚙ *prudence*

"Why aren't we all like that wise old bird?" Maybe we should speak less and hear more, like the owl.

A FEW MORE THINGS TO PONDER . . .

"All *work* and no play makes Jack a dull boy; all play and no work makes Jack a mere toy," has often been repeated as a proverb, and *love* is celebrated with poems about red roses and blue lavender.

Reader's Guide

Heads Up   *A little bit of extra help*

- Babies and toddlers like *Mother Goose* because the rhythms are pleasant and predictable, the characters are interesting, and the silly situations make them laugh. Most of all, they love the ones that are songs and have hand motions.
- As your child grows, encourage reciting these verses in unison as you read.

Dig Deeper   *Some things to think about after you read*

1. Which rhyme is your favorite?
2. Which picture is your favorite?
3. Can you remember how to keep the doctor away?
4. How did Yankee Doodle get to town?

There are many wonderful editions of *Mother Goose Rhymes*. The classic, old-fashioned versions are *Mother Goose,* illustrated by Kate Greenaway, and *Mother Goose,* illustrated by Arthur Rackham. Arnold Lobel, Tomie dePaola, and many others have taken fresh new approaches to these old poems.

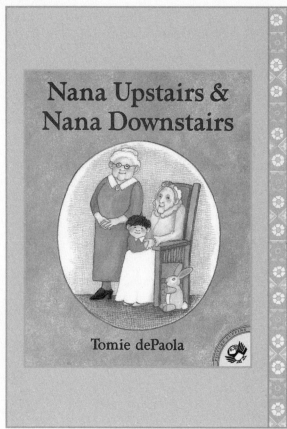

Nana Upstairs &
Nana Downstairs

Tomie dePaola

18

Nana Upstairs & Nana Downstairs

WRITTEN AND ILLUSTRATED BY TOMIE DEPAOLA

32 pages, 10 minutes of reading time
Ages 4 to 8

THEMES
*love, death, heritage, honesty,
respect, loss, hope*

The Story

Tommy was four years old and loved his Sunday visits to his nanas' house. Nana Downstairs was always cooking and Nana Upstairs, Tommy's great-grandmother, was always in bed, because she was so old. She offered him candy, told him stories, and was his very best friend. One day he woke to the news that she had died. Tommy was sad and missed her, but finally he found a way to try to understand this heartbreaking loss.

The Heart of the Book

There are so many beautiful themes in this tender story.

✸ *love*

Tommy's feelings for Nana Upstairs are best seen in the illustrations: he sits right next to her, leans on her arm, and gives her his bunny to hold. This is a sweet story of absolute love.

✸ *death*

When Tommy is told that his great-grandmother has died, he is too young to even know what that means. He only begins to comprehend it when he sees her empty bed. This is a painful but important step toward growing up for him.

✸ *heritage*

Regular Sunday visits, long hours with grandparents, and family home movies are all testimony to the value Tommy's parents placed in passing on their heritage.

A FEW MORE THINGS TO PONDER . . .

Mother approached Tommy with *honesty* about Nana Upstairs' death, and her *respect* for the *loss* of this most important person in his life meant that he was better able to grieve and heal. Tommy began to experience *hope* as he imagined the continued presence of his loved one.

Reader's Guide

Heads Up *A little bit of extra help*

- This is the story of a child's first experience with the death of a loved one. Be aware that it is very tender and very sad at times.
- This story was drawn from the author's own experience.

Dig Deeper *Some things to think about after you read*

1. Which pictures show that Tommy loves his nanas and that they love him?
2. Why did Tommy get angry at his brother's words?
3. What did Tommy think when he saw the first falling star?
4. How do you think he felt differently when he saw the second one?

Six million copies of Tomie dePaola's books have sold worldwide, and he receives nearly 100,000 fan letters each year.

19

The Very Hungry Caterpillar

WRITTEN AND
ILLUSTRATED BY
ERIC CARLE

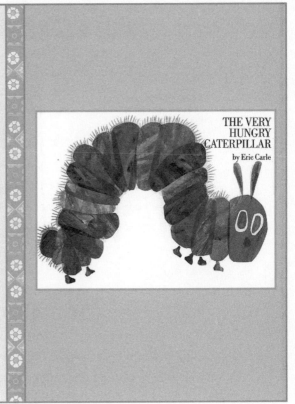

32 pages, 5 to 10 minutes of reading time
Infants to age 4

THEMES
growing up, nature, patience, respect

The Story

One lovely night, a little white egg is left on a leaf. When the egg hatches, out comes a little caterpillar, who is so very hungry that he eats everything in sight. Every day of the week he eats more and more until he is no longer little, but has grown into a "big, fat caterpillar." What will happen when he stops being hungry and wants to rest for a while?

A Page from *The Very Hungry Caterpillar*

On Saturday
he ate through
one piece of
chocolate cake, one ice-cream cone, one pickle, one slice of Swiss cheese, one
  slice of salami, one lollipop, one piece of cherry pie, one sausage, one cup-
  cake, and one slice of watermelon.
That night he had a stomachache!

The Heart of the Book

Young children begin to grasp the concepts of days of the week and counting as they enjoy this very popular book, and they might be shown a few other things, too.

⚙ *growing up*

As the days go by, eating makes the caterpillar grow. This is true for children, too.

⚙ *nature*

Days and nights pass. There are beautiful pictures of fruit and trees to look at and the caterpillar turns into a butterfly. Even babies can be entranced by the images of nature on these pages.

⚙ *patience*

It takes the caterpillar three whole weeks to turn into a butterfly. Sometimes we must be patient and wait for beautiful things to happen.

A FEW MORE THINGS TO PONDER . . .

A seed of *respect* for living creatures, even small ones, can be planted with this book, as well as an understanding of the cycles of life.

Reader's Guide

Heads Up   *A little bit of extra help*

- The hungry caterpillar leaves holes in the pages of the book that are just big enough for tiny fingers.
- As children grow, they can learn to count each item the caterpillar eats.

Dig Deeper   *Some things to think about after you read*

1. Where did the caterpillar come from?
2. Name some of the fruits and other foods he ate. What colors are they?
3. How many holes did he eat in the last leaf?
4. What is the house called that he built around himself?

The pictures in *The Very Hungry Caterpillar* are collages made by the author from colored papers.

20.

There Was an Old Lady Who Swallowed a Fly

WRITTEN AND
ILLUSTRATED BY
SIMMS TABACK

32 pages, 5 to 10 minutes of reading time
Ages 3 to 8

THEMES
creativity, curiosity, imagination

The Story

Peek into the hole in the front of the old lady to see what she's just swallowed. Then watch as she gets bigger, and bigger, and finally devours a horse and keels over. Along the way, there are lots of fun details to catch, like a disgusting recipe for spider soup and a poster for the missing dog ("last seen with old lady").

There was an old lady who swallowed a cat.
Imagine that! She swallowed a cat.
She swallowed the cat to catch the bird.
She swallowed the bird to catch the spider.
She swallowed the spider to catch the fly.
I don't know why she swallowed the fly.
Perhaps she'll die.

The Heart of the Book

This book is a terrifically funny read-aloud choice, with a couple of added benefits.

⚙ *creativity*
The extra lines on each page encourage children to make up their own rhymes to add to the fun.

⚙ *curiosity*
Eagerness to find out what happens to this unfortunate old lady keeps the pages turning.

A FEW MORE THINGS TO PONDER . . .
The holes cut in the pages, filled with whimsical drawings of each additional silly meal, help fuel the reader's *imagination*.

Reader's Guide

Heads Up *A little bit of extra help*

- This is an example of a "cumulative tale." There isn't much of a plot, and the story moves along by the addition of action and then repetition. Kids love these kinds of tales.
- Cumulative tales are great for early readers because they encourage learning through repetition.

Dig Deeper *Some things to think about after you read*

1. What are the pictures of on the back of the book?
2. Take a look at the old lady's face right before she eats the next thing. How does she look right after?
3. What are all the little items around the cow?
4. How does the old lady change as she swallows more and more things?

The text of *There Was an Old Lady Who Swallowed a Fly* is a well-known children's song. It is available in recorded form by many different artists.

21

Where the Wild Things Are

WRITTEN AND
ILLUSTRATED BY
MAURICE SENDAK

48 pages, 10 minutes of reading time
Ages 4 to 8

THEMES
*loneliness, forgiveness, obedience,
imagination, comfort*

The Story

Max has been making mischief and has talked back to his mother: he told her that he would eat her up. Now he's really in trouble. No supper for Max and off to bed he goes. Soon he grows a forest in his room with an ocean tumbling by and he sails off in his private boat to find a place more to his liking. It's fun where the wild things are, but Max gets a taste of what it is like trying to tame such rowdiness. He has second thoughts about leaving home, even if it is only in his head.

The Heart of the Book

Upon a closer look, this fantastic adventure of imagination touches on issues close to every child.

✦ *loneliness*

Max finds that his wild experiment doesn't make him feel any better. He is lonely without the someone who "loved him best of all." He just needed to leave home to find out how much he valued it.

✦ *forgiveness*

Max is angry about being punished and shows it with his untamed fantasy. The relief he feels at being forgiven for making mischief can be seen on his face when he finds his supper waiting in his room.

✦ *obedience*

Every child struggles with authority. Max creates a place where he is in control and must be obeyed. He can't handle such wildness for long, and perhaps imagines that this might be how his mother feels.

A FEW MORE THINGS TO PONDER . . .

Max's *imagination* has served him well by letting him create and control his world for a while. Max "let the wild rumpus start!" but soon wished to be back in the *comfort* of his loving home.

Reader's Guide

Heads Up   *A little bit of extra help*

- Sendak uses some fascinating techniques to convey Max's state of mind. Note how the pictures get larger as Max's fantasy grows, and then smaller again as he heads home.
- Notice the subtle difference in the colors in Max's bedroom at the beginning of the story and at the end. He comes home to a warmer place.

Dig Deeper   *Some things to think about after you read*

1. How does Max treat the wild things? How did he tame them?
2. Was he happy in the land where the wild things are?
3. Who brought supper into Max's room? Why?
4. Have you ever felt like being a wild thing?

Where the Wild Things Are is the first volume of a trilogy by Sendak that explores children's responses to strong emotions. The next two are *In the Night Kitchen* and *Outside Over There*.

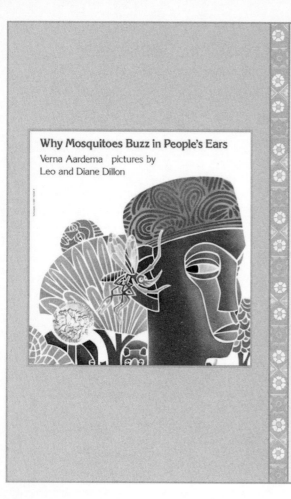

22

Why Mosquitoes Buzz in People's Ears

BY VERNA AARDEMA

Illustrated by Leo and Diane Dillon

28 pages, 10 minutes of reading time
Ages 4 to 8

THEMES
*fairness, responsibility, perseverance,
cooperation, justice*

The Story

The mosquito is so annoying. The iguana does all he can to block out the silly creature's nonsense, little knowing that his actions will start a chain of events that will affect every creature in the jungle. Things get so bad that even the sun doesn't come up and King Lion has to get to the bottom of things. The mosquito finally learns her lesson—or does she?

"Now, why won't he speak to me?" said the python to himself. "Iguana must be angry about something. I'm afraid he is plotting some mischief against me!" He began looking for somewhere to hide. The first likely place he found was a rabbit hole, and in it he went, wasawusu, wasawusu, wasawusu.

The Heart of the Book

This tale has real personality and some great value lessons as well.

⚙ *fairness*
King Lion gives each animal a chance to answer the charge against it.

⚙ *responsibility*
While each character admits to its own actions, finally the blame rests on the mosquito.

⚙ *perseverance*
This steady, predictable tale reflects a patient determination on the part of King Lion to resolve the matter.

A FEW MORE THINGS TO PONDER . . .
The animals of the jungle come together in *cooperation* to find out why the sun didn't rise. Finally *justice* is achieved when the mosquito gets "an honest answer."

Reader's Guide

Heads Up *A little bit of extra help*

- *Why Mosquitoes Buzz in People's Ears* is a wonderful example of a *pourquoi* tale (*pourquoi* means "why" in French). It is also a cumulative story because it progresses by way of repeating, then adding to the action.
- This book is great fun to read aloud because of the unusual sounds the animals make.

Dig Deeper *Some things to think about after you read*

1. Who is the wisest animal in the jungle?
2. Why was Mother Owl satisfied?
3. What did the mosquito do that caused the other animals to blame her for the sun not rising?
4. Why does the mosquito buzz in people's ears?

Verna Aardema also wrote *Bringing the Rain to Kapiti Plain,* a beautiful fable about Africa.

23.

Cars and Trucks and Things That Go

WRITTEN AND ILLUSTRATED BY RICHARD SCARRY

72 pages, 20 to 30 minutes of reading time
Ages 3 to 8

THEMES
*obedience, cooperation, helpfulness,
patience, courtesy*

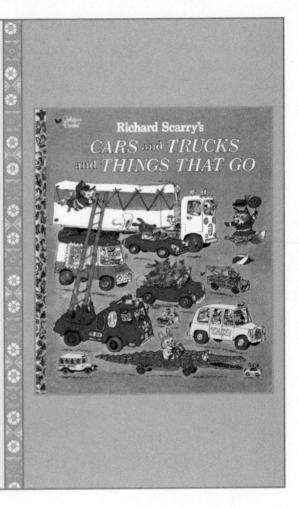

The Story

The Pig family is headed out for a fun excursion. Ma Pig packs up the picnic basket and they all climb in the little convertible to head to the beach. This should be an easy, relaxing trip, but it turns out to be quite complicated and very exciting. The runaway steamroller squashes three cars and the snow-covered watermelons almost catch up with the Pigs as they make their journey. There are hundreds of regular vehicles to look at, and lots of weird ones, too, like a cheese car and a swimming pool truck. Finally they get back home, no worse for wear except for a sunburn, with big surprises waiting on their doorstep.

A Page from *Cars and Trucks and Things That Go*

The Pig family is driving up into the mountains. It is getting colder. It is snowing. The road is icy. The pie truck skids off the road.

Mistress Mouse says it is time to put on snow chains.

Hey Pa! Wake up! Put on your snow chains! And please put the top up.

The Heart of the Book

This amusing book is packed with lots of valuable tidbits.

⊛ *obedience*
Dingo Dog had better learn to follow the rules or Officer Flossy will give him a ticket.

⊛ *cooperation*
The wheel loader loads the dump truck and the hook-and-ladder firefighters work with the rescue truck. These characters pull together to get the job done.

⊛ *helpfulness*
Mistress Mouse is always there to lend a hand. "She can fix almost anything."

A FEW MORE THINGS TO PONDER . . .
The Pigs must practice *patience* before they get to eat lunch, but even when they are in a hurry, they speak with *courtesy* to those around them.

Reader's Guide

Heads Up *A little bit of extra help*

- This book is great for toddlers and early readers, too. The whimsical vehicles and their friendly drivers keep children interested for long stretches.
- *Cars and Trucks and Things That Go* can be enjoyed just for the pictures.

Dig Deeper *Some things to think about after you read*

1. Were you able to track Goldbug all the way through the story?
2. What kind of trouble did Dingo Dog get into?
3. What is swarming all over the garbage dump?
4. Who calls for the fire trucks when Ladybug's car catches on fire?

Because children have so much fun matching the captions with the clever drawings, Richard Scarry's books are very popular with teachers as a tool for increasing vocabulary.

24

Cuadros de Familia/Family Pictures

WRITTEN AND ILLUSTRATED BY CARMEN LOMAS GARZA

32 pages, 20 to 25 minutes of reading time
Ages 6 to 12

THEMES
*family, work, resourcefulness, heritage,
community, encouragement,
cooperation, faith*

The Story

Carmen Lomas Garza grew up in a Texas town close to the Mexican border. From the time she was a young girl, she wanted to be an artist. She had a rich childhood, filled with relatives and friends, working and playing. Together they dreamed of the future. Later in life she looked back on her early years and painted pictures that vividly portray her fondest memories.

The Heart of the Book

The paintings, reproduced on every other page, tell this story as effectively as the text, which is presented both in English and Spanish.

⚙ *family*
The reader senses the strong, warm bond that holds Garza's family together. She grows and thrives in this safety and security.

⚙ *work*
There is hard work to be done, from laundry to making tamales, but it is part of the joy of being a family and growing up.

⚙ *resourcefulness*
Dinner is a chicken from the family's coop or a rabbit from the pen, along with vegetables from the garden. They grow their own oranges and pick cactus leaves to stir-fry for breakfast.

⚙ *heritage*
Every word and picture in this book reflects the respect the author has for her culture and history.

⚙ *community*
Carmen Lomas Garza grew up in Kingsville, Texas. Her memories are filled with the vibrant life of the town—parties, cakewalks, and holidays.

✺ *encouragement*

A testimony to the effect words and beliefs can have on a child, the author remembers that her mother "made up our beds to sleep in and have regular dreams, but she also laid out the bed for our dreams of the future."

A FEW MORE THINGS TO PONDER . . .

Cooperation makes any job easier and more pleasant: "In our family, everybody helps." Door-to-door Christmas visits and belief in the powers of the *curandera* (or healer) underline the importance of *faith* to this family.

Reader's Guide

Heads Up   *A little bit of extra help*

- Carmen Lomas Garza is highly regarded as a major Mexican-American painter.
- She focuses her art on simple acts of life that nourish the spirit. Notice how her simple but detailed pictures invite the reader to take a closer look.

Dig Deeper   *Some things to think about after you read*

1. How does this family have fun together?
2. What surprised Arturo in his grandmother's backyard?
3. In what way does this family express their faith in God?
4. Who encouraged the author to become an artist?

One of Garza's special talents is a unique form of *papel picado* (perforated paper). This is a traditional Mexican art form, usually used for creating banners and embroidery, in which intricate scenes are cut out of layers of tissue paper.

25.

Curious George

BY H. A. REY

64 pages, 10 to 15 minutes of reading time
Ages 4 to 7

THEMES
*obedience, independence, friendship,
patience, determination*

The Story

Cute little George the monkey lived in the jungle and was very happy there. But when he saw a yellow hat lying on the ground, he couldn't help himself. He grabbed it and put it on his head. That curiosity got George caught and shipped overseas with the nice man who owned the yellow hat, and that is the beginning of George's adventures. No matter how hard he tries, George just can't keep from getting into trouble. The fun is seeing how he'll get out.

A Page from *Curious George*

The man with the big yellow hat
put George into a little boat,
and a sailor rowed them both
across the water to a big ship.
George was sad, but he was still
a little curious.

The Heart of the Book

George is a plucky little character who does what most kids would like to do: break free for a while, have adventures, and be rescued if they get in trouble.

⚙ *obedience*
"George promised to be good. But it is easy for little monkeys to forget." Lots of children will relate to this problem.

⚙ *independence*
George senses so few limitations that he actually tries to fly like the seagulls. Almost always he displays a spirit that is totally free.

⚙ *friendship*
The man in the yellow hat feels affection for George, and rescues him time after time. He's the perfect friend for a monkey who gets himself into such predicaments.

A FEW MORE THINGS TO PONDER . . .

The picture of *patience*, George's friend never seems to tire of getting the monkey out of trouble. George's **determination** to explore new things leads him onto a ship, into the sea, up in the air, into jail, and off to the zoo.

Reader's Guide

Heads Up   *A little bit of extra help*

- The bright primary colors on these pages help keep a child's eyes focused on the story.
- Take the time to point out the details in some of the drawings.

Dig Deeper   *Some things to think about after you read*

1. George was happy in his home in Africa, but he seems to adjust well to his new surroundings. Point out a picture of a happy George.
2. Why is it so easy for George to walk on the telephone wire?
3. How does the man in the yellow hat show that he likes George?
4. Do you think George will stay in the zoo?

- H. A. Rey once had a job selling bathtubs up and down the Amazon River.
- Hans and Margret Rey left Europe in 1940 to escape the Nazi invasion of Paris. The only things they brought with them to America were their coats and their book manuscripts.

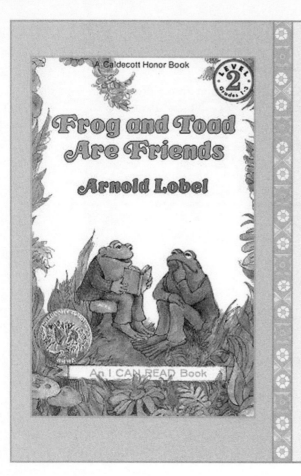

26

Frog and Toad
(series)

WRITTEN AND
ILLUSTRATED BY
ARNOLD LOBEL

64 pages each
10 to 15 minutes of reading time
Ages 5 to 8

THEMES
*generosity, fear, individuality,
encouragement, helpfulness*

The Story

Frog and Toad spend almost every day together, doing the things friends do. They are very alike, and very different at the same time. Frog loves the seasons and Toad does, too, but Toad must be coaxed from his warm bed to enjoy the weather. They both like stories, but Toad mostly listens. He has a hard time thinking up stories. Sometimes they are cross, but they find a way to make things right. Sometimes they cause each other trouble, but always they are glad that they are best friends.

The Heart of the Book

Who wouldn't like to have a friendship like this one? Frog and Toad like each other, respect each other, and have a good time sharing life.

⊛ *generosity*
"Frog, Frog," cried Toad, "taste these cookies that I have made." These characters love to share.

⊛ *fear*
Frog and Toad find that they can face frightful things better if they team up and face them together.

⚙ *individuality*

Toad is introspective and a little grumpy, with a big, big heart. Frog is impulsive and adventuresome. They look at each day in different ways and are the happier for it.

A FEW MORE THINGS TO PONDER . . .

Toad would be a much sadder creature without Frog's *encouragement* and Frog is always grateful for Toad's *helpfulness*. Like all good friends, they need each other.

📖 Reader's Guide

Heads Up *A little bit of extra help*

- These books have been proven to be perfect for children who are learning to read. The rhythm, use of pictures, and length of words and stories make beginning reading fun.
- Children feel more grown-up as they are able to read the chapters in these books by themselves.

Dig Deeper *Some things to think about after you read*

1. In *Frog and Toad Are Friends,* what did Frog do to make Toad feel better about the mail?
2. On the first day of spring, what did Frog want to do? What did Toad want to do?
3. Name some ways Toad is generous with Frog.
4. The two friends want to find out if they are brave in *Frog and Toad Together.* What do they find out?

Arnold Lobel said that his stories came from remembering how he felt as a child. Long segments of his childhood were spent in hospitals, where he was confined because of a series of illnesses.

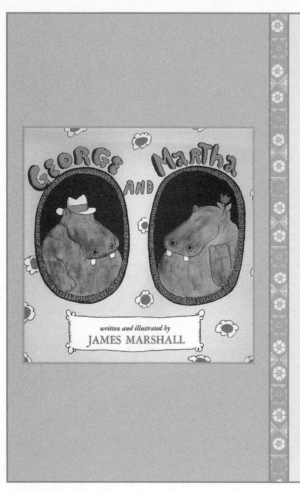

27

George and Martha

(series)

WRITTEN AND ILLUSTRATED BY JAMES MARSHALL

32 pages each, 5 minutes of reading time
Ages 5 to 8

THEMES
honesty, encouragement, confidence, privacy, friendship, respect, forgiveness

The Story

Martha wears beautiful skirts with bold, giant patterns on them that go all the way to the floor. George has a huge gleaming gold front tooth and likes to play practical jokes. These two hippos are absolutely best friends. They go to the cinema, bake gifts for each other, ride the Ferris wheel, and make each other laugh. Of course, once in a while, like all friends, they get hurt feelings or have misunderstandings. They always make up, though, because that's what best friends do, especially two great hippos like George and Martha.

A Page from *George and Martha One Fine Day*

"Boo!" cried George.

"Have mercy!" screamed Martha.

Martha and her stamp collection went flying.

"I'm sorry," said George. "I was feeling wicked."

"Well," said Martha. "Now it's my turn."

"Go ahead," said George.

"Not right away," said Martha slyly.

Suddenly George found it very difficult to concentrate on what he was doing.

"Any minute now, Martha is going to scare the pants off me," he said to himself.

The Heart of the Book

James Marshall has done a marvelous thing with these stories. George and Martha come to the page complete with all their flaws and idiosyncrasies, and the reader gets to watch gleefully as the two friends deal with each situation.

✿ *honesty*
George pours his pea soup into his loafers, hoping to spare Martha's feelings, but he could have just told her the truth. It turns out that she doesn't like pea soup, either.

✿ *encouragement*
"That's what friends are for," George tells Martha. "They always look on the bright side and they always know how to cheer you up."

✿ *confidence*
When George praises her performance on the tightrope, Martha's confidence returns.

⚙ *privacy*

The bathtub ends up on George's head because he doesn't respect Martha's privacy.

A FEW MORE THINGS TO PONDER . . .

George and Martha help the reader think about the true value of *friendship*, as they try and try again to *respect* each other and show *forgiveness*.

📖 Reader's Guide _____

Heads Up *A little bit of extra help*

- These stories present a lovely opportunity to discuss all kinds of common small problems with the young reader.
- Stop often as you read aloud together and ask for reactions to the interesting dilemmas presented in each book.

Dig Deeper *Some things to think about after you read*

1. George pastes a silly picture over the mirror in *George and Martha*. Why?
2. What kind of personality do you think Martha has? Is she clever? Is George a good prankster?
3. Martha tries to get George to cut down on eating sweets in *George and Martha Tons of Fun*. How does she do this? Does it work?
4. In *George and Martha One Fine Day*, why can't George eat his dessert?

There are seven books in the *George and Martha* series: *George and Martha*, *George and Martha Encore*, *George and Martha Rise and Shine*, *George and Martha One Fine Day*, *George and Martha Tons of Fun*, *George and Martha Back in Town*, and *George and Martha Round and Round*.

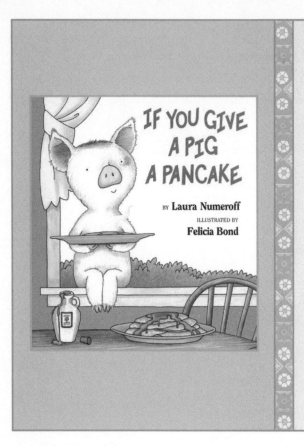

28

If You Give a Pig a Pancake

BY LAURA NUMEROFF

Illustrated by Felicia Bond

32 pages, 5 to 10 minutes of reading time
Ages 2 to 6

THEMES
creativity, responsibility, generosity, individuality

The Story

Share your pancakes with the little piglet at the kitchen window—she's too cute to ignore. It might complicate your day, but it is so much fun to see what she asks for next.

The Heart of the Book

The little girl tries to keep up with the requests of the pig, and the reader catches some clever themes along the way.

❋ *creativity*

From the first page, we can see that the little piglet is happy to let her imagination run free. Every move she makes prompts her to do something unexpected.

❋ *responsibility*

The perfect illustrations show us a girl who is enjoying her new job of keeping up with (and cleaning up after) a surprise visitor.

❋ *generosity*

She shares her syrup, her bubbles, her tap shoes, and anything else the piglet asks for, and she makes a new friend.

A FEW MORE THINGS TO PONDER . . .

This little pig positively bursts with personality. She has her own idea about what she wants to explore and is a picture of *individuality*.

Reader's Guide

Heads Up *A little bit of extra help*

- Notice that the emotions of this story are conveyed in the pictures. We know how the characters feel just by looking at the illustrations.
- Take the time to look for details in the pictures.

Dig Deeper *Some things to think about after you read*

1. How did the little pig get to the house?
2. How did she get up to the window?
3. Why was she looking for a suitcase? She never finds it. Why?
4. By the end of the story, who is tired?

It might be fun to have the author's other books like this one on hand for the moment when your child says, "More, please." The titles are *If You Give a Mouse a Cookie* and *If You Give a Moose a Muffin*.

29.

Little Bear (series)

BY
ELSE HOLMELUND MINARIK

Illustrated by Maurice Sendak

64 pages each, 20 minutes of reading time
Ages 3 to 6

THEMES
*comfort, creativity, patience, imagination,
growing up, generosity*

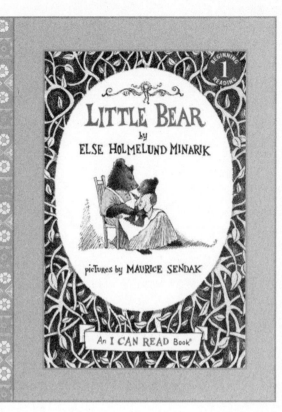

The Story

Little Bear is a little bit brave and a little bit timid. He likes adventures, but he also likes to come home. In fact, Little Bear is just like most children. His gentle Mother Bear is always there to love him and take care of him. Whether he has been off on a trip to the moon or trying to throw a nice party for his friends, Little Bear finds that he likes it best in his own snug home.

A Page from *Little Bear*

Little Bear climbed to the top of a little hill,
and climbed to the top of a little tree,
a very little tree on the little hill,
and shut his eyes and jumped.
Down, down he came with a big plop,
and down the hill he tumbled.
Then he sat up and looked around.
"My, my," he said.
"Here I am on the moon.
"The moon looks just like the earth.
Well, well," said Little Bear.

The Heart of the Book

These sweet little stories deliver some simple messages.

⚙ *comfort*

Little Bear's mother holds him on her lap and he feels safe and loved. "For you are my little bear, and I know it," she says.

⚙ *creativity*

"Let me see what we have. We have carrots and potatoes, peas and tomatoes." Little Bear doesn't have a cake, so he makes birthday soup.

⚙ *patience*

Mother Bear knows what her little one needs, but serenely waits for him to find out for himself.

❀ *imagination*

All of Little Bear's bedtime wishes for castles and clouds are dreams of fantasy.

A FEW MORE THINGS TO PONDER . . .

Experimenting with his environment is part of ***growing up*** for Little Bear. He is a little anxious about having no birthday cake because he wants to show ***generosity*** to his friends.

Reader's Guide

Heads Up *A little bit of extra help*

- Notice how the longer sentences are broken into segments to make the story easier for new readers.
- *Little Bear* is a fine choice for bedtime reading.

Dig Deeper *Some things to think about after you read*

1. Did Little Bear need the hat and the coat and the snow pants his mother made for him? Why not?
2. Why did Little Bear make birthday soup?
3. Name two things Little Bear wished for at bedtime.

Little Bear marks a significant achievement in early reader books. It uses a limited vocabulary, but with its format it appeals to the young reader's desire to be challenged. It is actually four stories in four chapters.

30.

Magda's Tortillas

BY
BECKY CHAVARRÍA-CHÁIREZ

Illustrated by Anne Vega

32 pages, 10 to 12 minutes of reading time
Ages 4 to 8

THEMES
*encouragement, individuality, creativity,
heritage, respect, growing up,
responsibility, patience*

The Story

Magda had been waiting for this day. She was finally seven years old and big enough to make tortillas with her *abuela* (grandmother). Patiently, her *abuela* shows her every step, from scooping the dough to using the rolling pin. Magda is sure she can make beautiful, perfectly round tortillas for her birthday party later, but as the morning goes by and she tries time after time, the best she can do is roll out funny-looking tortillas shaped like stars or bananas. She is tempted to give up, but Abuela lovingly urges her to keep going. Magda learns that there is something better than being perfect. It is being unique.

The Heart of the Book

Magda's Tortillas is a wonderful picture of a close-knit loving family.

⚙ *encouragement*

Magda's grandmother places more importance on her granddaughter's effort than she does on doing the job a certain way.

⚙ *individuality*

They are not perfectly round and they don't look like Abuela's, but Magda's tortillas are prized for their uniqueness. Each person is unique, too, and should be valued as an individual.

⚙ *creativity*

"My Magda is a tortilla artist." This little girl begins to feel the satisfaction of making something from scratch.

⚙ *heritage*

In this family, tradition is passed from one generation to the next in the natural context of the home, the best way to learn it.

⚙ *respect*

It is obvious that Magda's family members have been taught to respect their parents and grandparents. It is nice to see that Abuela also respects Magda's feelings.

A FEW MORE THINGS TO PONDER . . .

Marking this stage of *growing up* is important for Magda. It is another step toward the *responsibility* of adulthood. Doing anything well requires *patience,* and Magda finds that there is a reward for her perseverance.

Reader's Guide

Heads Up   *A little bit of extra help*

- The text of this book is split into two parts. The top half of the page is in English and the bottom half is the exact same story told in Spanish. It presents an excellent multicultural viewpoint.
- Bilingual picture books are great learning tools for anyone of any age who is trying to learn a language.

Dig Deeper   *Some things to think about after you read*

1. What does the Spanish word *abuela* mean?
2. How do you suppose Magda's grandmother learned to make tortillas?
3. Do you think Abuela was disappointed in Magda's first try? How do you know?
4. What is Magda going to learn to do when she turns eight?

Becky Chavarría-Cháirez has worked as a radio commentator on the Dallas National Public Radio affiliate.

31.

Officer Buckle and Gloria

WRITTEN AND
ILLUSTRATED BY
PEGGY RATHMANN

32 pages, 10 minutes of reading time
Ages 4 to 8

THEMES
cooperation, individuality, encouragement,
helpfulness, loneliness

The Story

The students at Napville School aren't very interested in Officer Buckle's safety talks. They yawn and throw paper planes, sometimes even snore. Officer Buckle is a nice enough guy, just maybe a little dull—that is, until he brings along Gloria, his new police dog. Suddenly his young audience becomes fascinated and entertained by his presentation. They even send thank-you letters to the surprised policeman. Of course, when he figures out that Gloria is putting on a show for the kids behind his back, Officer Buckle vows to stop his safety talks forever. Maybe some of his friends can change his mind.

The Heart of the Book

Officer Buckle and the other characters in this story learn some lessons, and so will the reader.

⚙ *cooperation*

Officer Buckle tries to do the safety talk alone and so does Gloria, but it's a flop. They need each other.

⚙ *individuality*

Gloria has a natural gift for entertainment and Officer Buckle is very good at safety tips. He learns to appreciate Gloria's unique contribution.

⚙ *encouragement*

The students (especially Claire) cheer up the discouraged policeman with their letters, and convince him to come back to the school.

A FEW MORE THINGS TO PONDER . . .

Officer Buckle displays real *helpfulness* by taking time to talk to the kids about safety tips (there are some great ones tacked all over these pages). He and Gloria don't like the feeling of *loneliness* they have when they try to do the job alone.

📖 Reader's Guide

Heads Up *A little bit of extra help*

- Notice how the understated text makes the wild pictures even funnier in *Officer Buckle and Gloria*.
- Take the time to catch the details. Look at the safety notes and the awards on Officer Buckle's walls.

Dig Deeper *Some things to think about after you read*

1. What is Officer Buckle's favorite letter that comes in the mail? Why?
2. How do you think Gloria feels as she watches the ten o'clock news with her buddy, Officer Buckle?
3. What is Officer Buckle good at? How about Gloria? Why do they make a great team?

Peggy Rathmann got the idea for this book from an old home video in which a family dog was sampling the food on the table behind the hostess who was narrating the video.

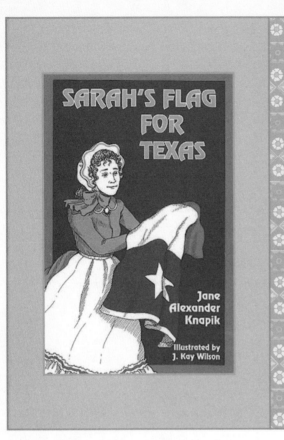

32

Sarah's Flag
for Texas

BY

JANE ALEXANDER KNAPIK

Illustrated by Jo Kay Wilson

110 pages, 2 to 3 hours of reading time
Ages 9 to 13

THEMES
history, faith, duty, freedom, adversity

The Story

Sarah Bradley moved from Kentucky to Texas with her parents and seven of her siblings in 1822, after her father was given one of the first land grants for the new colony. She was about ten years old when they started their new life, and by 1834 was twenty-three and helping to carry the load of running the four-hundred-acre ranch. Her widowed mother, Liza, and her children watched with concern as the future of Texas was put in jeopardy by the dispute between the leader of Texas, Stephen Austin, and Santa Anna, the new president of Mexico. Uncertainty and unrest were in the air, with Austin put in prison and the new settlers left with no leadership.

Amid all this uncertainty, Sarah falls in love with an intelligent and thoughtful man named Archie Dodson and they begin a family many miles from her old home. When Austin returns from prison with the decision to call Texans to arms against Mexico, Sarah's husband tells her that he must go fight. With the encouragement of the women around her, Sarah fashions a banner for the men of his little troop to carry with them to war: red and blue with a lone star.

A Page from *Sarah's Flag for Texas*

"Liza, what have you done here?" Papa asked, astounded. He paused to try to comprehend what had happened. Three hoes, two axes, a small garden plow, and two large packets of seeds lay on the ground around him. That same ground had been so empty when he went to bed.

Finally, he rushed over to his wife and picked her up in a mighty hug. He twirled her around before finally setting her down again. Above the happy sounds coming from other family members, Papa's voice came through with a statement the family would forever quote. "Liza, you are an amazin' woman, a surprisin' woman!" he said, then hugged and kissed her soundly again.

The Heart of the Book

The men and women who settled in Texas in the 1800s saw many changes in the political climate around them. They were the kind of people who learned to think for themselves and protect one another.

✸ *history*

This account of the creation of one of the original designs of the Texas state flag is a good way to learn a simple version of that state's turbulent history.

⚜ *faith*

"A day never passed that some member of the family didn't find occasion to quote the Scriptures." Faith was an important part of the Dodson family's view of life and the Bible was one of the only books they had.

⚜ *duty*

These early pioneers were dedicated to one another and to their commitment to the new territory they were attempting to tame. Even though Archie and the other men are anxious about leaving their families at home, they believe it is right to do their part in what might be a long war.

A FEW MORE THINGS TO PONDER . . .

Stephen Austin is "sad but emphatic" when he calls his fellow Texans to arms. He believes their *freedom* is at stake because Mexico will not abide by the constitutional agreement. The first settlers were well-acquainted with *adversity*. Sarah sees the gravestones along the road and is reminded of the hardship in their lives.

📖 *Reader's Guide* _____

Heads Up *A little bit of extra help*

* This book is based on a true story.
* To show the setting of this story, use a map to trace the Brazos River from the Gulf Coast through the middle of Texas.

Dig Deeper *Some things to think about after you read*

1. How did Sarah's father die?
2. Why are horses so important to a Texas rancher?
3. Why does Sarah go out to sit on the old wagon bench when she needs to make a decision about Archie?

4. How does Sarah get the idea for the flag colors? Why does she put one white star on it?

5. Why does Archie have to stay behind when he wants to go rejoin the troops?

- The Bradleys took their eight children about a thousand miles from Christian County, Kentucky, to their new homestead in Texas.
- Santa Anna's father was Spanish and his mother was French. He was the president of Mexico eleven times.

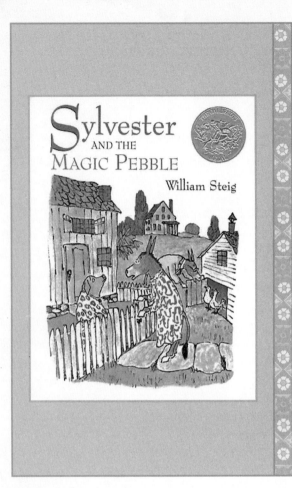

33

Sylvester and the Magic Pebble

WRITTEN AND ILLUSTRATED BY WILLIAM STEIG

30 pages, 10 to 15 minutes of reading time
Ages 5 to 7

THEMES
*family, encouragement, hope,
wealth, fear, courage*

The Story

Sylvester Duncan, the donkey, liked to collect unusual rocks, ones of different shapes and sizes. When he found a perfectly round, bright red shiny pebble, he was very excited, and then absolutely astonished to find that it had magic powers. If he made a wish while holding it in his hoof, the wish came true. Before he could get it back home to his mother and father, he was frightened by a hungry lion and accidentally turned himself into a rock. Sylvester learns a "hard" lesson: his warm home and loving parents are better than all the magic in the world.

A Page from *Sylvester and the Magic Pebble*

He was frightened. If he hadn't been so frightened, he could have made the lion disappear, or he could have wished himself safe at home with his father and mother. He could have wished the lion would turn into a butterfly or a daisy or a gnat. He could have wished many things, but he panicked and couldn't think carefully. "I wish I were a rock," he said, and he became a rock.

The Heart of the Book

These animal characters are endearing, all dressed up in clothes and walking on their hind legs, and their story leaves lasting impressions of important values.

⚙ *family*
Mr. and Mrs. Duncan have created a warm, loving home for their little family. Being separated from his parents makes Sylvester's plight all the more poignant.

⚙ *encouragement*
"Let's cheer up," Mr. Duncan says to his wife. He tries to help her be happy even though Sylvester is gone. This is a sweet picture of kind support.

⚙ *hope*
It doesn't seem possible that Sylvester will ever be saved from his terrible situation. Still, a tiny hope lives in him and his parents. The instant that hope is spoken, their wish comes true.

⚙ *wealth*
The magic pebble is put away after it brings Sylvester back because the Duncans are not interested in wishing for things that would make them rich. With the family reunited, they have all they need and want.

A FEW MORE THINGS TO PONDER . . .

It is Sylvester's *fear* that makes him not able to think clearly, therefore accidentally wishing for disaster. His parents show *courage* in their attempt to go on living their lives without their dear child.

Reader's Guide

Heads Up   *A little bit of extra help*

- Point out that the illustrations for *Sylvester and the Magic Pebble* were created with watercolors.
- This story is a good example of a fable, which is a short story with a moral or lesson.

Dig Deeper   *Some things to think about after you read*

1. What does Sylvester plan to do with the magic pebble?
2. How do we know that Sylvester is gradually losing hope?
3. How did Sylvester turn into himself again?
4. Can you think of any other ways the magic pebble could have changed Sylvester back into a donkey?

William Steig also wrote the popular children's book *Shrek*.

34.

The Snowy Day

WRITTEN AND
ILLUSTRATED BY
EZRA JACK KEATS

32 pages, 5 minutes of reading time
Ages 1 to 5

THEMES
*curiosity, nature, growing up,
resourcefulness, comfort*

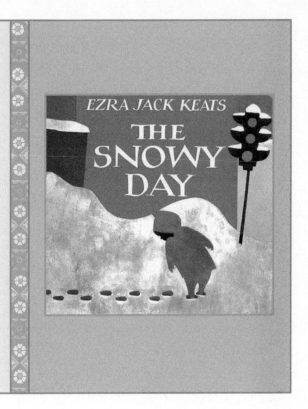

The Story

L ittle Pete wakes up to find that an overnight snowfall has blanketed the city. He bundles up and runs out to spend the day discovering what kind of fun can be had in this new, white world. The sidewalks have a smooth, fresh coating on them, perfect for footprints. There are tall drifts for the make-believe mountain climber, and a smiling snowman to create. Nothing is more fun than a snowy day—unless, as Pete finds out, it's a second one.

A Page from *The Snowy Day*

He pretended he was a mountain-climber.

He climbed up a great big tall heaping mountain of snow and slid all the way down.

He picked up a handful of snow—and another and still another. He packed it round and firm and put the snowball in his pocket for tomorrow.

The Heart of the Book

This book is vibrant in color and emotion, celebrating the simple enjoyment of a season in a little boy's life.

⚙ *curiosity*

The snow is irresistible to Pete. Any child who has ever awakened to a world covered in white, or ever dreamed of such a morning, will relate to his wonder at the sight.

⚙ *nature*

Children remember seasons. *The Snowy Day* gives the reader a chance to imagine and begin to connect winter to a particular time of year.

⚙ *growing up*

Pete is big enough to go out and play by himself, but finds out he is still too little to play with the big boys when he gets knocked down by a snowball.

A FEW MORE THINGS TO PONDER . . .

Pete is learning how to use his own *resourcefulness* by entertaining himself all day in the snow. The calm illustrations and his mother's care for her son are a *comfort* to a young reader.

Reader's Guide

Heads Up *A little bit of extra help*

- This is a great snuggle-up-and-read-aloud book and goes well with a cup of hot chocolate.
- Children like to look at the pictures in *The Snowy Day* over and over again after the reading is through.

Dig Deeper *Some things to think about after you read*

1. Where does Pete live? How do you know?
2. What are some things that Pete did on the snowy day?
3. Why was the snowball no longer in Pete's pocket?
4. What would you do with a snowball if you wanted to keep it?

- *The Snowy Day* was one of the earliest mainstream children's books to feature a black child as the main character.
- Ezra Jack Keats created these illustrations using cutouts, watercolors, and collage.

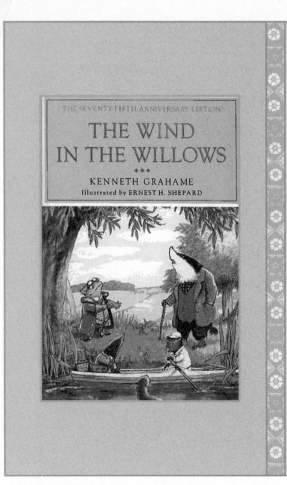

35

The Wind in the Willows

BY KENNETH GRAHAME

Illustrated by Ernest H. Shepard

240 pages, 12 chapters
5 to 6 hours of reading time,
or 30 minutes per chapter
Ages 7 to 11

THEMES
*nature, loyalty, prudence, generosity,
friendship, flaws*

The Story

Mole is doing a little spring-cleaning in his underground home, but springtime beckons and out he goes into the world above. He meets Ratty, soon to be his best friend. Ratty even asks Mole to share his home for a while, and so it happens that Mole is introduced to all the wonders of the river, the woods, and the community of friends he will come to cherish.

Through their adventures, Mole, Ratty, Badger, and Toad find out many things about themselves and one another. Mole is very much like a little child, eager for adventure, but somewhat rambunctious. Often this puts him on the receiving end of wise Ratty's advice and instruction. They try not to trouble the revered Badger, but it takes all three of them to rescue Toad, who is mesmerized by his latest hobby, motorcars, and will not stop boasting about his exploits, even when he has behaved in a less than admirable manner.

Whatever the predicament, these friends can count on one another. This story celebrates the joys of nature, the loyalty of comrades, and the promise of adventure that comes with every new day.

A Page from *The Wind in the Willows*

The Mole was tremendously interested and excited, and followed him eagerly up the steps and into the interior of the caravan. The Rat only snorted and thrust his hands deep into his pockets, remaining where he was.

It was indeed very compact and comfortable. Little sleeping bunks—a little table that folded up against the wall—a cooking-stove, lockers, bookshelves, a bird-cage with a bird in it; and pots, pans, jugs and kettles of every size and variety.

"All complete!" said the Toad triumphantly, pulling open a locker. "You see— biscuits, potted lobster, sardines—everything you can possibly want. Soda-water here—baccy there—letter-paper, bacon, jam, cards and dominoes—you'll find," he continued, as they descended the steps again, "you'll find that nothing whatever has been forgotten, when we make our start this afternoon."

"I beg your pardon," said the Rat slowly, as he chewed a straw, "but did I overhear you say something about *'we,'* and *'start'* and *'this afternoon'?*"

The Heart of the Book

⚙ *nature*

Kenneth Grahame obviously believed in the value of the natural world. These chapters are filled with some of the most beautiful descriptions of nature ever written for children.

⚙ *loyalty*

All along, these friends are unfailingly loyal to one another. It may be difficult at times to stand up for conceited Toad or come to the rescue of impetuous Mole, but they stand with each other through the bad and the good.

⚙ *prudence*

Mole learns about prudence, or carefulness, in one unwise trip to the Wild Wood, but for Toad the lesson is almost impossible to grasp. The story teaches that it is better to use caution than to be sorry in the end for a bad decision.

A FEW MORE THINGS TO PONDER . . .

"But come along; come into the kitchen. There's a first-rate fire there, and supper and everything." The Badger is not hesitant to share what he has with his unexpected visitors on a cold night, and indeed, *generosity* is how all these characters show their *friendship* for one another. They are animals that often act like humans, and it is the way they deal with their own *flaws* and those of their friends that gives us a glimpse of ourselves.

📖 *Reader's Guide* _____

Heads Up *A little bit of extra help*

• It might be fun to look for pictures in an encyclopedia of the kinds of animals who are the characters in *The Wind in the Willows,* especially the ones that might be unfamiliar to the reader: a stoat, a badger, a ferret, or a mole.

- Be aware that the "adventure" chapters alternate with the calmer chapters; this pace helps the reader understand the characters and setting.

Dig Deeper *Some things to think about after you read*

1. The animals in *The Wind in the Willows* act like humans most of the time. Why do you think the author chose to tell this story with animals instead of people?
2. Which characters are contented with their lives and which are not?
3. How do we know that Mole, Badger, and Ratty have real affection for Toad?
4. Does Toad learn a lesson? What is it?

- The setting for *The Wind in the Willows* is very much like the area around Cookham Dene, the English village in which the author was raised by his grandmother.
- Chapter five's title, "Dulce Domum," means "Sweet Home" in Latin.

36

Tomás and the Library Lady

BY PAT MORA

Illustrated by Raul Colón

32 pages, 10 to 15 minutes of reading time
Ages 5 to 8

THEMES
*encouragement, fear, resourcefulness,
heritage, helpfulness, education*

The Story

It is a long way from Texas to Iowa. Tomás and his family make the trip in their old car every summer because their job for the season is to pick corn. Tomás and his brother do their part to help with the long, hot workdays, and sometimes they get the treat of hearing their grandfather tell his old stories.

Then comes the day when a very special lady shows Tomás a whole new world of distant places and fascinating adventures—the library. He is transported by the stories and finds a sanctuary there in the shelves. Soon he finds that he is good at telling these stories to his family in the evenings.

This is the true story of a little boy whose life was changed forever because of a kind librarian. It is a simple testimony to the difference one act of helpfulness can make.

A Page from *Tomás and the Library Lady*

Tomás sat down. Then very carefully he took a book from the pile and opened it.

Tomás saw dinosaurs bending their long necks to lap shiny water. He heard the cries of a wild snakebird. He felt the warm neck of the dinosaur as he held on tight for a ride. Tomás forgot about the library lady. He forgot about Iowa and Texas.

The Heart of the Book

Tomás remembered the details of this summer in his life, because it was at this time that he discovered the power of words and learning.

⚙ *encouragement*
Tomás was fortunate to have a grandparent who urged him toward books and to find a librarian willing to give him the help he needed to get started.

⚙ *fear*
The library's "tall windows were like eyes glaring at him." Tomás felt what most people feel when confronting an unfamiliar experience. He needed help to conquer his feelings and go inside.

⚙ *resourcefulness*
Far away from home and familiar surroundings, Tomás has the desire and the will to find what he is looking for in the library.

✻ *heritage*

Like so many Americans, Tomás lives in a family of two cultures and two languages. His family keeps its rich culture alive through stories and traditions.

A FEW MORE THINGS TO PONDER . . .

The library lady's *helpfulness* was a comfort to Tomás, and the key to the new door opening for him. He took the first step toward the love of learning that is the basis of a good *education*.

Reader's Guide _____

Heads Up   *A little bit of extra help*

- Point out that this is a true story.
- Notice how the illustrations add to the feeling of the hot summertime in which the story is set.

Dig Deeper   *Some things to think about after you read*

1. Why was Tomás afraid to go in the library?
2. What were some of the Spanish words Tomás taught the library lady?
3. How do we know that it is a hot summer in Iowa?
4. Do you think Tomás felt differently on the way home than he did on the way to their summer job? How?

This story is based on the real experience of Tomás Rivera. Rivera's lifelong love of learning led him from a farm worker's childhood to being a leader in education and a chancellor of the University of California at Riverside.

37.

Amazing Grace

BY MARY HOFFMAN

Illustrated by Caroline Binch

32 pages, 10 minutes of reading time
Ages 5 to 8

THEMES
*imagination, encouragement, confidence,
prejudice, individuality*

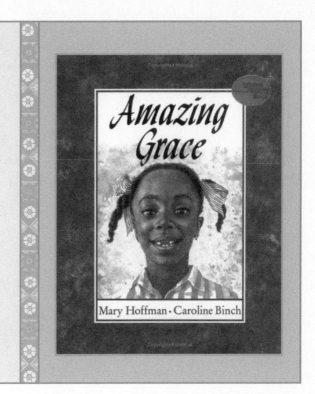

The Story

Grace had quite an imagination. She listened with fascination as her nana told her stories from her childhood. She pretended she was the main character in a favorite storybook, or simply made up tales out of her own head. Acting out stories was her favorite thing to do, even if she had to play all the parts.

When Grace found out that her class at school was going to do the play *Peter Pan,* she knew at once that she wanted to audition for the starring role, but her friends objected. She's black. She's a girl. She simply cannot play Peter Pan, they told her. With the help of her family, Grace must decide if she can fly outside the limits and make her dream come true.

A Page from *Amazing Grace*

"That one is little Rosalie from back home in Trinidad," said Nana. "Her granny and me, we grew up together on the island. She's always asking me do I want tickets to see her Rosalie dance—so this time I said yes."

After the ballet Grace played the part of Juliet, dancing around her room in her imaginary tutu. I can be anything I want, she thought.

The Heart of the Book

Grace is accustomed to the freedom she finds in books and the safety that surrounds her at home. It is within the security of her family that she develops her strong character.

✿ *imagination*
Grace pretends she is a pirate, or a spider, or an explorer, and in this way uses creative fantasy to bring the world to her.

✿ *encouragement*
Ma and Nana could see that Grace doubted her decision to audition for the play. She needed their help to see how strong she really was.

✿ *confidence*
When the other students saw Grace's performance, they knew she was going to get the part. Her strong belief in herself and her ability shone through.

A FEW MORE THINGS TO PONDER . . .
Limitations are often based on *prejudice* and preconceived ideas. A person's *individuality* is her most valuable asset.

Reader's Guide

Heads Up   *A little bit of extra help*

- It might be fun to watch a video of *Peter Pan* before you read this book.
- Notice how the pictures reinforce the emotions that are present in each scene.

Dig Deeper   *Some things to think about after you read*

1. How do the pictures in the book show that Grace is part of a loving family?
2. What is the most interesting character Grace pretends to be?
3. Why would Grace want to play the part of Peter Pan?
4. Why did seeing Rosalie in the ballet encourage Grace?

- Mary Hoffman is from England, but her book *Amazing Grace* is most popular in the United States.
- There is a Grace doll based on the character in Mary Hoffman's books.

Books for Intermediate

and Independent Readers

38.

Esperanza Rising

BY PAM MUÑOZ RYAN

272 pages, 4 to 5 hours of reading time
Ages 8 to 13

THEMES
adversity, gratitude, dignity,
hope, compassion, freedom,
determination, work, wealth

The Story

On the day before her thirteenth birthday, Esperanza Ortega's life is beautiful, filled with laughter and love and luxury. Her father, a kind and influential man, owns the large ranch in Mexico where they live, and Esperanza is his special, spoiled only child. As her father is out tending to his land, he is killed by bandits, and Esperanza's mother is given an ultimatum by their evil relatives: marry the disgusting but powerful uncle or be left penniless. Mama creates another option. She takes Esperanza and escapes in the middle of the night to America with her loyal servants, leaving Esperanza's grandmother, Abuelita, behind because she is not well enough to travel. It is a difficult adjustment for all of them, but it is most painful for Esperanza. This girl, who has never held a broom or helped in a kitchen or even bathed herself, wakes up in a California migrant workers' camp living in a tiny shack with her mother and strangers.

As might be expected, Esperanza gets very little sympathy from the workers in the camp, and as she is trying to adjust to her new life, another blow is dealt. Mama comes down with valley fever and Esperanza finds herself in charge of their survival. She clings to the memory of her father, tries to remember all her grandmother's proverbs, and finds within herself the raw material it takes to rise to the challenge.

A Page from *Esperanza Rising*

Esperanza looked from Mama to Carmen to Hortensia. She was amazed at how easily Carmen had plopped herself down and had plunged into intimate conversation. It didn't seem correct somehow. Mama had always been so proper and concerned about what was said and not said. In Aguascalientes, she would have thought it was "inappropriate" to tell an egg woman their problems, yet now she didn't hesitate.

"Mama," whispered Esperanza, taking on a tone she had heard Mama use many times. "Do you think it is *wise* to tell a peasant our personal business?"

Mama tried not to smile. She whispered back, "It is all right, Esperanza, because now we are peasants, too."

Esperanza ignored Mama's comment. What was wrong with her? Had all of Mama's rules changed since they had boarded this train?

The Heart of the Book

In her safe home as a child, values were planted in Esperanza. The words of her father and mother, the instruction and proverbs of her grandmother become a part of her life, but—as is the case with all of us—the meaning of wise words changes as life changes. Esperanza comes full circle to begin to understand the words she has been hearing all of her young life.

✹ adversity

In order to grow, a person must endure hardship. "There is no rose without thorns." Esperanza is accustomed to a comfortable and lovely life. She is young and has been shielded from the ugly side of the world around her, and of course assumes that there will always be roses. The thorns that she must endure are necessary to produce a mature young woman.

⚙ gratitude

The poor woman on the train says, "I am poor but I am rich. I have my children. I have a garden with roses, and I have my faith and the memories of those who have gone before me. What more is there?" For a girl rich in material things, it is impossible to believe that this can be enough, but by the end of the story, Esperanza is grateful for these things.

⚙ dignity

Esperanza and her friends in Mexico look forward to their *quinceañeras,* their presentation parties, after which they will be old enough to marry, "rising to the positions of their mothers before them." Esperanza finds that it is possible, even necessary, to have dignity without position, but it takes quite a struggle for her to learn this.

⚙ hope

"We are like the phoenix," said Abuelita. "Rising again, with a new life ahead of us." When her grandmother says this, Esperanza imagines that their new life will be the same life she has had. But soon she must hold on to another instruction from Abuelita: "Do not be afraid to start over." "Esperanza" means "hope," and she begins a life that takes her on a deeper, richer journey, always looking forward. As the Mexican proverb at the beginning of the book says, "He who falls today may rise tomorrow."

A FEW MORE THINGS TO PONDER . . .

The poor woman is happy to give what she has when she sees the needs of others. Esperanza has so changed by the end of the book that she becomes full of *compassion,* too. Miguel tells Esperanza, "In Mexico we stand on different sides of the river." He is a ranch hand and she is the daughter of the landowner, but he longs to have *freedom* in America, to be whatever he has the *determination* to be. There is pride in the *work* these people do in the fields and in their humble homes, and Esperanza learns what real *wealth* is. "The rich person is richer when he becomes poor, than the poor person when he becomes rich."

Heads Up *A little bit of extra help*

- Point out how the "mountains and valleys" in the crocheting reflect the family's experiences.
- Esperanza's father loves the land. Watch for indications that this feeling is passed on to his daughter.
- Notice the different ways Esperanza's mother acts with dignity.
- Note that each chapter is named for a fruit or vegetable, and think about why.
- Look for phrases or thoughts that express the novel's theme of hope.

Dig Deeper *Some things to think about after you read*

1. What are the "thorns" or challenges in Esperanza's life?
2. In what situations are we shown that Esperanza is self-centered? How do we know she has changed at the end?
3. How do Papa's words, "Wait a little while and the fruit will fall into your hand," become encouragement to Miguel?
4. Why does Esperanza dislike Marta so much? Are Marta's grievances reasonable?
5. Why is it important for Alfonso and Miguel to carry the rose cuttings with them from Mexico?
6. How does Mama's illness affect Esperanza's determination and work ethic?
7. By the end of the story, is there still a "deep river" that runs between Miguel and Esperanza?

Pam Muñoz Ryan was born and raised in California's San Joaquin Valley. During hot summers, she spent most of her time riding her bike to the library. It became her favorite place to go because her family didn't have a swimming pool and the library was air-conditioned. That's when she began to love books.

39.

Love That Dog

BY SHARON CREECH

112 pages, 1 hour of reading time
Ages 8 to 12

THEMES
confidence, creativity, education,
courage, encouragement

SHARON CREECH
WINNER OF THE NEWBERY MEDAL FOR *WALK TWO MOONS*

LOVE
THAT
DOG

a novel

The Story

Jack's teacher, Mrs. Stretchberry, has asked her students to react to the poetry she reads to them in class. They do this in their class journals and Jack's journal has a very clear message: Jack doesn't like poetry. It's for girls.

School is school, though, and Jack has assignments to complete, so he begins to write a few words. At first, he is reluctant to let anyone know who is the author of these spare verses Mrs. Stretchberry tacks to the board, but gradually he gets more willing.

Jack's writing reveals the beginning of a fascination with the mysterious power of words. Even if the meaning of a poem is lost on him, "at least it sounded good" in his ears, and he stretches a little further. When he finds the courage to invite a favorite poet to speak to his class, he is rewarded with an inspiring visit from Walter Dean Myers, and the lesson is complete. Jack finds that he does have something to say and poetry gives him a way to say it.

A Page from *Love That Dog*

SEPTEMBER 21

I tried.
Can't do it.
Brain's empty.

SEPTEMBER 27

I don't understand
the poem about
the red wheelbarrow
and the white chickens
and why so much
depends upon
them.

If that is a poem
about the red wheelbarrow
and the white chickens
then any words
can be a poem.
You've just got to

make
short
lines.

OCTOBE R 4

Do you promise
not to read it
out loud?
Do you promise
not to put it
on the board?

Okay, here it is,
but I don't like it.

So much depends
upon
a blue car
splattered with mud
speeding down the road.

The Heart of the Book

This little book packs a big punch. The reader is drawn into Jack's transformation even as he is taught how to read and appreciate poetry.

🌼 confidence

"I tried. Can't do it. Brain's empty." Jack thinks at first that he has nothing to write about. He doesn't even understand the poems his teacher is reading aloud to the class. One step at a time, as he writes and sees his poems on paper, his confidence grows.

🌼 creativity

Most children respond to creativity in any area. "My brain was pop-pop-popping," Jack says upon reading an especially imaginative poem, and he goes on to create his own word picture. Early attempts at creativity are imitations, but this is a great way for Jack to find his own voice.

🌼 education

Love That Dog has so much to say about good teaching. Mrs. Stretchberry's methods are very clever and very effective. Because she cares about her students and pays attention to their words, Jack is given the help he needs to express himself.

A FEW MORE THINGS TO PONDER . . .

As Jack's confidence grows, so does his *courage*. First he allows his name to be put on his poem, then he agrees to write the famous poet, and finally he finds the courage to write the poem about his dog. *Encouragement* from his teacher and classmates helps Jack feel safe to write about personal things.

📖 Reader's Guide _____

Heads Up   *A little bit of extra help*

- The poems Mrs. Stretchberry uses in her class are included at the end of *Love That Dog*. Read them before you read the book.
- Notice the signs that Jack might like poetry, even though he says he doesn't.

- Notice this author's very effective way of revealing the teacher's approach to teaching.
- The creative way this book is organized is part of its appeal. Try reading it aloud.

Dig Deeper *Some things to think about after you read*

1. Why doesn't Jack want his name attached to his poems?
2. What are the early indications that Jack might be a poet?
3. How does this book make poetry seem interesting?
4. Sharon Creech is good at writing like a boy in class. What are some examples of this?
5. What was the "best best BEST news ever"?
6. Sometimes writing about difficult things can make them feel less painful. Does Jack feel better after writing about his dog, Sky?

- Walter Dean Myers is an author best known for his stories about young urban blacks.
- Like Mrs. Stretchberry in *Love That Dog,* Sharon Creech knows something about being in a classroom. The author spent eighteen years teaching and writing in Europe.

40.

A Year Down Yonder

BY RICHARD PECK

144 pages, 2 to 3 hours of reading time
Ages 9 to 12

THEMES
self-sufficiency, family, community,
growing up, generosity, patriotism

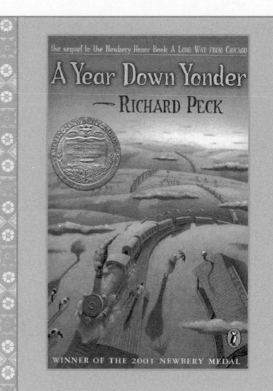

The Story

Mary Alice is not happy about getting on the train and going to Grandma's house. For one thing, she has to leave her family behind. To make it worse, she'll be gone a solid year. Times are tough in 1937 Chicago. Her father has lost his job, and he and Mary Alice's mother are moving into a rented room just big enough for the two of them. Her brother, Joey, is off planting trees for the government. Mary Alice will have to go to a new school in a backwoods town with no friends and no family—except Grandma. That's a scary thought. Fifteen-year-old Mary Alice has spent the last few summers with Grandma and she knows the old woman is well-known for her schemes in the little Illinois town where she lives. It's going to be a long year.

To Grandma, the right end always justifies sneaky, even illegal means, and Mary Alice finds herself an accomplice in most of Grandma's capers. Moonlit raids, tricks on old and young fools, and old-fashioned blackmail are all tools in Grandma's apron pocket, mostly used to outwit the unsuspecting and help the unfortunate. The months are full of adventure and change, and Mary Alice comes to the end of the year as a girl much wiser in the ways of romance and homegrown justice, and with a deep appreciation for the lessons taught by Grandma in her little Illinois town.

A Page from *A Year Down Yonder*

By now I was standing next to the porch just below her, bug-eyed to see what she was getting away with. Even I knew the next customer, Mr. L. J. Weidenbach, the banker. He was a big, sleek, slack-mouthed man as tight with money as Grandma herself.

He didn't wear a Legion cap. He may have been too old for the war. Anyway, he'd stayed home and made money. He held out a very thin dime.

Grandma looked at that dime like she'd never seen one. Her eyes were circles of astonishment. "That won't do it, L.J.," she said, loud. Mr. Weidenbach winced. The porch sagged with customers of his bank.

"What do you want from me, Mrs. Dowdel?" he muttered.

"From you I wouldn't say no to a five-dollar bill," Grandma said, louder than before. "If you can get the bootlace loose from around your wallet. The boys who fought at the front didn't count the cost."

The Heart of the Book

Because *A Year Down Yonder* is so entertaining, it might be easy to miss the messages in the wild adventures of Mary Alice and her grandmother. Little by little Mary Alice becomes more aware of the wisdom and motivations in Grandma's actions, and this changes and enriches her life.

⚙ *self-sufficiency*

Jobs are scarce and money is tight in 1937 America, but Grandma Dowdel always seems to have enough. She hatches plenty of ingenious schemes to find good things to eat or animal skins to trade, and her shed is filled with stuff she puts to use in a hundred different ways. She even wears Grandpa's old clothes. "I often wonder what she'd buried Grandpa Dowdel in. She seemed to wear every stitch he'd owned," Mary Alice muses. She doesn't waste a thing, and Mary Alice begins to make this valuable trait a part of her own way of doing things.

⚙ *family*

Especially during hard times, family bonds can strengthen and grow. Mary Alice carries with her the support and love of her parents and brother, and by the end of this story she has developed a connection with her grandmother that will continue through the years. She begins to recognize some things about herself that are like Grandma, and she feels her grandmother's love for her, even though it is never expressed in words. Many times we learn through time and experience that family ties are the strongest of all.

⚙ *community*

The people in this little town in the country are very aware of one another's business. Grandma even recognizes a horse and knows it is not with its rightful owner. And when the postmistress runs naked out of the house and down the street, the news travels faster than she does. This close communication isn't good news to Mary Alice, who would like to suffer out her year in obscurity, but she finds that with the bad comes the good: Grandma also knows who needs rescuing after a tornado strikes, and when to use that very stolen horse to put Mary Alice's enemy in her proper place. Living in community means you might not have much privacy, but you do have true friends.

A FEW MORE THINGS TO PONDER . . .

A different Mary Alice gets on the train back to Chicago at the end of the year. Several months out of the city living with Grandma have given her the gift of a little time for *growing up*. She couldn't have a better teacher for learning the art of anonymous charity and wisdom in *generosity*. Grandma's behavior at the turkey shoot is an example of both, and also is a poignant picture of the *patriotism* in America's heartland.

Reader's Guide

Heads Up   *A little bit of extra help*

- Point out how we are shown that Mary Alice has been brought up to respect her relatives.
- Grandma can certainly take care of herself. Notice each example of how she does this.
- Look for ways that the people in this small community take care of one another.
- This era was sometimes called "the Roosevelt recession" because there weren't enough jobs to go around. Find examples of hard times in this little town.

Dig Deeper   *Some things to think about after you read*

1. Describe a situation in which Grandma surprised Mary Alice with a gift. Do you think Mary Alice felt loved by her grandmother? In what ways does Mary Alice protect her?
2. Is it easier to get to know your neighbors in a small town than it is in a big city? Why?
3. How do we know Mary Alice is close to her family?
4. Are you surprised at Grandma's tricks and escapades? Would you like to stay at her house?

5. When did Mary Alice use a trick or two of her own?
6. Grandma is wise in the ways of romance, too. How does she get involved in the town's matchmaking?

In the story, Mary Alice's brother went to work for the Civilian Conservation Corps. This program provided jobs planting trees for young men who were out of work during and after the Depression.

41.

Because of Winn-Dixie

BY KATE DICAMILLO

184 pages, 1 to 2 hours of reading time
Ages 8 to 13

THEMES
*inclusion, friendship, first impressions,
living with uncertainty, flaws,
compassion, understanding*

The Story

Right in the middle of the grocery store's produce section, ten-year-old India Opal Buloni adopts a dog. She has to give him a name on the spot, so she names him Winn-Dixie, the name of the store and the only words that jump into her mind at the time.

Winn-Dixie is unusual. He grins and then he sneezes. He makes friends with everyone he meets, even Gertrude the parrot. No one can resist the big, old, rough-looking dog. Opal's daddy takes him in as one of the "Less Fortunate," and then, to keep him from howling, even lets him sit in church on Sundays. Little old Miss Block breaks her own rule and allows him in the library while she tells her fascinating family stories. He's the best friend Opal has ever had.

"Just about everything that happened to me that summer happened because of Winn-Dixie," says Opal, and she's right. She finds out some things about the mother who abandoned her, makes friends with the "witch" in the neighborhood, and comes up with a way to bring the whole community of lonely, hurting people together. By the end of that eventful season, Opal and her preacher father have found their way to forgiveness, healing, and hope.

A Page from *Because of Winn-Dixie*

"We'll have to keep an eye on him," the preacher said. He put his arm around Winn-Dixie. "We'll have to make sure he doesn't get out during a storm. He might run away. We have to make sure we keep him safe."

"Yes sir," I said again. All of a sudden it was hard for me to talk. I loved the preacher so much. I loved him because he loved Winn-Dixie. I loved him because he was going to forgive Winn-Dixie for being afraid. But most of all, I loved him for putting his arm around Winn-Dixie like that, like he was already trying to keep him safe.

The Heart of the Book

Opal wonders about her absent mother and feels distant from her daddy. The characters that come into her life bring her the important lessons she needs.

✺ *inclusion*
Opal is lonely living in Naomi, Florida. She's new in town and is the preacher's daughter. She tells God that the other kids "probably thought I'd tell on them to the preacher for every little thing they did wrong." More than anything, she wants to be included, but she finds she has to be the first to reach out. She has to try hardest with Dunlap and Stevie Dewberry, but in the end she finds they need a friend, too.

⚙ *friendship*

Winn-Dixie jumps straight into Opal's heart and becomes her true friend. The little girl can tell that the dog needs her, and Opal surely needs a companion. It even seems that Winn-Dixie can communicate with Opal, encouraging, commiserating, and leading her to the people who can help her most.

⚙ *first impressions*

Miss Fanny Block seems strange because she locks herself away in her library, but inside she has a treasure chest of wonderful stories to tell. Amanda seems like a snob but she is grieving silently. Otis has spent some time in jail but he is gentle and a magical musician. When the characters are given the chance to express who they really are, it becomes clear that they have a wealth of gifts to offer. Opal learns from Gloria Dump to "remember, you can't always judge people by the things they done. You got to judge them by what they are doing now."

⚙ *living with uncertainty*

Like the Littmus Lozenge, life tastes sweet and sad, all at the same time. Each character is trying to hold on to something that is already gone. "I believe, sometimes, that the whole world has an aching heart," Gloria tells Opal. In the end, how we accept loss and how well we allow ourselves to heal determine how deeply we can value what we have today.

A FEW MORE THINGS TO PONDER . . .

Gloria Dump has tied all of her empty bottles to the branches of a tree in her backyard to keep away the ghosts of all the things she has done wrong. She is almost blind but uses the tree to remember the mistakes she has made. Being honest about *flaws* makes it easier to live with them in others and in ourselves and is the first step toward *compassion*. The next step is *understanding*. When Opal finds out why Amanda is sad, and how much her daddy misses her mother, she is no longer distant, but responds with kindness.

Heads Up   *A little bit of extra help*

- Notice how the setting for each scene aids the progress of the story.
- Watch for indications that Opal's outlook is changing.
- Point out how the author handles the subject of the elderly being isolated.

Dig Deeper   *Some things to think about after you read*

1. How does Winn-Dixie help Opal make friends?
2. Otis has been in prison. Is he dangerous?
3. The Littmus Lozenge has an unusual effect on the people who eat it. How does it make them feel and why?
4. Why does Opal call her father Preacher? When does she begin to call him Daddy?
5. What is Winn-Dixie afraid of?
6. Name ten things you know about someone you love.
7. Why does Opal say that her heart "doesn't feel empty anymore. It's full all the way up," at the end of the story?

There are subtle Bible references in this story: The name of the town is Naomi, like Ruth's mother-in-law in the Old Testament. Also, Gloria asks Opal not to judge, but to forgive.

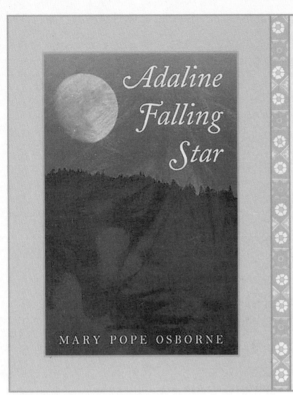

42.

Adaline Falling Star

BY MARY POPE OSBORNE

170 pages, 2 to 3 hours of reading time
Ages 9 to 12

THEMES
*faith, prejudice, abandonment, trust,
loneliness, death, determination*

The Story

Adaline Falling Star was the daughter of Kit Carson and his Arapaho wife, who died when Adaline was small. In this story, she is eleven years old when her father leaves her with his cousin in St. Louis so he can join an expedition led by "The Pathfinder," Lieutenant John C. Fremont. She begs not to be left behind but, with a promise to return for her, Kit Carson hurries off to meet up with the famous explorer.

From the minute she is introduced to Cousin Silas and his family, Adaline is misunderstood and labeled. She decides to say no words at all to the people in this family, all of whom think she is a "savage." When she hears them talk of trying to wash away her "Indian stain," she responds with a menacing growl. What they don't know is that she can read and write. She is filled with curiosity about scientific things and keeps books hidden to read in secret.

Finally believing that her father has left her behind for good, she runs away, knowing that it will be better to die in the wilderness than to be chained up in an asylum.

Her struggle with loss and loneliness makes her stronger and determined to survive. A fierce, frightened Adaline finds a new companion in a mongrel dog, and together they fight their way toward her old home.

A Page from *Adaline Falling Star*

We drag ourselves out of the water. The dog gives a good shake and rubs his nose in the grass while I haul the canoe into dry brush.

My buckskins are soggy and heavy as I pull on my moccasins. All of a sudden, I feel like my legs are about to give out. I have to sit.

The dog crouches nearby, snapping at the air, trying to catch the mosquiters and flies.

Dang critters are still thirsty for my blood, but I can't think about them now. I got something worse to ponder. I got a fever from my cuts.

The Heart of the Book

There is beautiful poetry in this book. Adaline's conversations with herself and with Dog reflect her upbringing among expressive people. At the end of her dangerous journey she finds new understanding and the security she is looking for.

✸ *faith*

"Watchman, tell us of the night, what its signs of promise are." These words and words of other hymns are a comfort to Adaline, who learned them from Rosalie, the cook back at the fort. Adaline has been taught Indian beliefs from her mother and Christianity from others in her life. Even as her fascination with science begins to affect how she understands her world, still she leans on the things she cannot see to give her strength.

⊛ *prejudice*

Cousin Silas and his family assume that Kit is embarrassed about having a half-breed daughter and decide she is only good for helping them with the chores. Adaline longs to join the class at school but, once she is aware of the family's animosity toward her, she is too proud to let them know she is not a mute. This only adds to the problem. The family's pre-formed opinions about Indians keep them from showing her the love she desperately needs.

⊛ *abandonment*

Adaline's fear of being left in St. Louis is intensified by the fact that she is motherless. She clings to her "Ma doll," and waits to hear her mother's words come to her in the night. So great is her despair when she believes she has been abandoned by her father that she cuts herself with a knife and is sorry to find she wakes up alive.

⊛ *trust*

"I give you my word I'll be back for you," Adaline's father tells her. She clings to his words and believes them until the entire expedition comes back without him. Later she learns her trust was not misplaced and that her father was never going to leave her behind forever.

A FEW MORE THINGS TO PONDER . . .
Adaline experiences such acute *loneliness* after her father leaves her, and this pain pushes her to extremes, like pretending muteness and snarling like an animal. She copes with her mother's *death* by imagining the life her mother is living in the Land-Behind-the-Stars. The little girl's *determination* to find her father and demand answers is what pushes her to survive.

📖 Reader's Guide _____

Heads Up *A little bit of extra help*

• Adaline, the book's main character, is born into an Arapaho family on Horse Creek in Colorado. It might be interesting to read a little about the Arapahos in an encyclopedia before you start reading *Adaline Falling Star*.

- Be sure to start with the Author's Note at the beginning.
- Look for the author's use of flashbacks to describe Adaline's life before St. Louis.
- Point out that Kit Carson, Adaline's father, was one of America's most famous frontiersmen.

Dig Deeper   *Some things to think about after you read*

1. Why can't Adaline go on the expedition with her father?
2. Why does she decide to pretend she's mute?
3. What are the "fruits of civilization," according to Doc Hempstead?
4. Caddie has a special bond with Adaline. Why is this so?
5. Two times Adaline chops her hair off and cuts herself with a knife. What prompts her to do this?
6. How does Dog save Adaline's life?
7. Under what circumstances does Adaline lose her "Ma doll" and then her bag of "possibles"?

- John Charles Frémont, "Pathfinder" in the story, was a famous American explorer. He was also the first candidate of the Republican Party to run for the office of president of the United States, and he was married to Jessie Benton, the daughter of Missouri Senator Thomas Hart Benton.
- Here are just a few places named after Kit Carson:
  Carson City, the capital of Nevada
  Kit Carson Peak in southern Colorado
  Carson National Forest in northern New Mexico
  Carson Pass in the Sierra Nevada Mountains

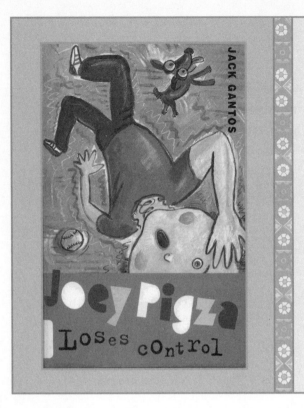

43.

Joey Pigza Loses Control

BY JACK GANTOS

195 pages, 3 to 4 hours of reading time
Ages 9 to 13

THEMES
*choice, trust, self-esteem, honesty,
responsibility, obedience, prejudice*

The Story

Joey can barely keep himself from bouncing around the car. His mom is taking him to his dad's house for a few weeks and Joey's hyperactive mind has a million questions. Carter, Joey's dad, claims to have quit drinking and gotten a job, but Joey's mom has her doubts. Joey has Attention Deficit/Hyperactivity Disorder (ADHD), but has a newfound stability now that he is on his "good meds." He is developing an ability to think first, act later. Still, he has bad moments, like last week, when he put a dart through his dog's ear. Joey has heard all the bad things about his dad, about his drinking and his insane behavior. He knows he is going to have a tough time with mean, growly Grandma, who lives with Carter, but he's trying to believe that it could all turn out great.

One look in his dad's eyes and Joey gets the picture: "He was *wired*. No doubt about it." As the days go on, things get crazy. Carter never stops talking, peels his nicotine patch off so he can smoke, and guzzles beer for breakfast. Grandma cheats Joey out of his money so she can buy cigarettes, even as Joey pushes her around in a grocery cart with her oxygen tank attached. When Carter says Joey doesn't need medicine and flushes it all down the toilet, Joey starts feeling and acting like "the old wired Joey" again and learns the hard way that it is up to him to find his way back to safety.

A Page from *Joey Pigza Loses Control*

"I'm not sending you because *I* like him," she replied. "I'm sending you because *you* might like him and because I think—not with my heart—that it is a good thing for you to have a relationship with your father. And now that he claims to have stopped drinking and has a job and has gone to court to get some visitation, I'm sending you to him because I think it's the right thing to do. But don't ask me how I *feel* about all this."

"How do you *feeeeel*?" I asked, and leaned forward and pressed my smiley face into her shoulder.

"Don't go there," she said. "I really don't want to feel anything about all this."

"Mom and Dad, sitting in a tree, k-i-s-s-i-n-g!" I sang again with my head bouncing as if my neck was a big spring.

"Now, Joey," Mom said, lifting one hand off the steering wheel and pushing me back to my side. "Get serious. Don't cling to the notion that me and him are going to get back together. No way is that going to happen, so just let it go and focus on your relationship with your father. You have six weeks with him. Figure out what you want from this guy before you get there. Give it some thought because he can be, you know, wired like you, only he's *bigger*."

The Heart of the Book

What an extraordinary experience it is to bounce around in Joey Pigza's mind. His sweet nature and good intentions are all there, but it takes great effort and his "good meds" patch for him to focus on one thing at a time. When his father takes over because of his own selfish needs, Joey is forced to learn some hard lessons.

✿ *choice*

Joey's main conflict is with himself. He knows the right thing to do, but he doesn't know how to resist his father's words and choose for himself. One bad decision leads to another until he sees that it is up to him to make a good choice and call for help.

✿ *trust*

Joey wants to trust his dad and spends most of his time giving Carter one chance after another, knowing he is putting himself in danger. It takes a little time for Joey to give up this hope, but finally he finds that his basic instincts are correct. He can rely only on the people in his life who have proven themselves to be worthy of trust.

✿ *self-esteem*

"The *little business* she referred to made me hang my head because it was all my fault . . ." Joey is familiar with the feeling of being in trouble. Before this visit to his dad's, he had been learning how to manage his behavior so he could feel good about himself and not hurt others. He does not want his father to destroy this new self-esteem.

✿ *honesty*

The characters in this story tell the truth to one another with one exception: Carter, Joey's dad. He convinces himself with lies, and attempts to drag everyone else along with him to his make-believe new life. Joey feels panic at every turn, as he ignores his own integrity and begins to lie to his mother and to himself.

A FEW MORE THINGS TO PONDER . . .

In the end, each person must take *responsibility* for his choices, good or bad. Joey is just a kid, and a kid with ADHD. He finds out how important *obedience* is, and how essential it is to obey boundaries set by the right person. Through the words on the page we are given a fascinating view into Joey's hyperactive mind. Understanding his struggle helps to combat the *prejudice* against these common disorders in children and adults.

Reader's Guide

Heads Up   *A little bit of extra help*

- Point out how the author uses sentence structure to show how Joey thinks.
- Notice how Joey tries to drown out anything he doesn't want to hear.
- Note the ways the author shows us signs of addiction in these characters.
- Look for the turning points in Joey's decision-making.

Dig Deeper   *Some things to think about after you read*

1. Joey has never played baseball but he is a good pitcher. How is that possible?
2. Why does Joey agree to go bungee jumping and do other scary things with his dad? Is he glad he makes these decisions?
3. How do their addictions interfere with Grandma's and Carter's ability to show love to Joey?
4. This story is hilarious and sad. What is your favorite funny scene? Your favorite sad scene?
5. Who is Joey's best friend?
6. Why can't Grandma leave Carter's house, even though she is unhappy there?
7. How can a book like *Joey Pigza Loses Control* help us understand people who behave in unusual ways?

- ADHD stands for Attention Deficit/Hyperactivity Disorder.
- This book is the sequel to *Joey Pigza Swallowed the Key*.

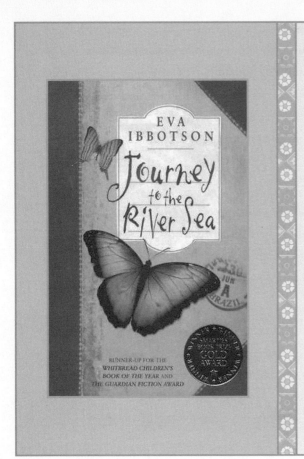

44.

Journey to the River Sea

BY EVA IBBOTSON

Illustrated by Kevin Hawkes

295 pages, 5 to 6 hours of reading time
Ages 12 to 15

THEMES
*abandonment, freedom, prejudice,
conformity, nature, environment,
courage, education*

The Story

Maia sits alone on the top of the mahogany library steps at her boarding school and reads about the Amazon rain forest. She has just been told that she is to go live with the Carters, relatives of hers in Manaus, Brazil, and though she is a little afraid, she is mostly excited. She will have a home and a family, and since her parents died two years earlier, this is a warm and inviting thought. It is 1910, and living in the jungle couldn't be more different from her present life in a London school for girls, but her hunger for adventure makes the change welcome. Soon she is not just reading about the Amazon but sailing down it accompanied by her new governess, the stern Miss Minton, on their way to the Carters' house and a new life.

The shock of her new situation quickly hits her. Mr. and Mrs. Carter, along with their hateful twin girls, are greedy, cruel people, locked away in their disinfected house, intent on remaining "untainted" by the native environment. Maia and Miss Minton must use creative tactics to survive in this dreadful family, and along the way they find themselves falling in love with the magic of Brazil's native culture, making unlikely friends and helping two boys hatch a plan to escape a trap and give themselves a fresh start.

A Page from *Journey to the River Sea*

When Furo disappeared through the narrow channel of rushes the silence seemed overwhelming—yet she heard the noise of the water lapping the *Arabella,* the whirr of the hummingbirds' wings, the dog yawning. It was as though sounds had been freshly invented in this secret place.

Finn led her to the door of the hut. "My father built it and we lived here whenever we weren't away on collecting trips. I still can't believe he isn't coming back, though it's four months since he was drowned."

"Do you see him sometimes?" Maia asked—and he turned sharply because she seemed to have read his thoughts. "I see mine. My father. Not a ghost or an apparition . . . just him."

The Heart of the Book

It is easy to tell the good guys from the bad guys in *Journey to the River Sea*. The characters are interesting and engaging, and it is fun to be carried along by the intrigue. A closer look at this exciting adventure story reveals some interesting themes.

✵ *abandonment*
Maia, Clovis, and Finn are orphans. Miss Minton and Professor Glastonberry have been left all alone in the world. "We are *all* going home." These are the last words of the book and a clear statement of what the chief characters hope for in *Journey to the River Sea*.

✿ *freedom*

Mrs. Carter exercises her power to choose by creating a highly restricted home. Finn is willing to take a great risk in order to remain in the jungle, while Clovis is desperate to get back to the confines of civilization. The native Brazilians maintain their own independence, even while working for the plantations. Each is willing to sacrifice to have his version of freedom.

✿ *prejudice*

Because the native people are different from them, the Carters treat them as though they are inferior. Maia approaches them as equals, as she does Clovis, Finn, and the new people she meets in Manaus, and is given the gift of friendship in return.

✿ *conformity*

Miss Minton's corset is a wonderful symbol of the restrictions that have been put upon her in her life. She is ordered to wear it by Mrs. Carter and keeps it on even in the heat, but when she decides to break out of the life she has been living, she throws it overboard. In this story, conformity is good only if it is freely chosen.

✿ *nature*

The natural world is the source of much magic and mystery, and all of the central characters in *Journey to the River Sea* are affected by it. Finn and his father, Professor Glastonberry, Miss Minton, and Maia are all willing to take great risks to study it. The natural world is left standing when the Carters, who have nothing but disdain for it, must leave.

A FEW MORE THINGS TO PONDER . . .

Maia has been living in a healthy *environment* all of her life. When she moves into an unhealthy one, she knows the difference and fights against it with all the *courage* that comes from her strong belief in a just cause. All through the story the value of a well-rounded *education* is emphasized. Knowledge is seen as a good thing, while ignorance leads to disaster.

Reader's Guide

Heads Up *A little bit of extra help*

- Note on a map just how far the Amazon is from England.
- Consider all the subjects Maia has been taught—languages, music, and more.
- Part of the story includes a skeleton of a giant sloth. Be ready with a picture of that prehistoric animal.

Dig Deeper *Some things to think about after you read*

1. Why is Maia so willing to go to Brazil?
2. How do the servants know that Maia wants to be their friend?
3. Some of these characters are very happy in the jungle and some are miserable. Why?
4. What is in Miss Minton's heavy trunk? Why is it so precious to her?
5. What is Mr. Carter's odd hobby? How does it contribute to his bankruptcy?
6. The greed of Gwendolyn and Beatrice makes them even more vicious than usual. How does their selfishness lead to the house fire?
7. Is Clovis wrong for choosing to live at Westwood?

- The scientific name for giant sloths is "megatherium." They were prehistoric animals almost as big as elephants, with huge claws.
- The theater in the story is now called the Amazonas Opera House. It opened in 1896 and was built in the shape of a harp.

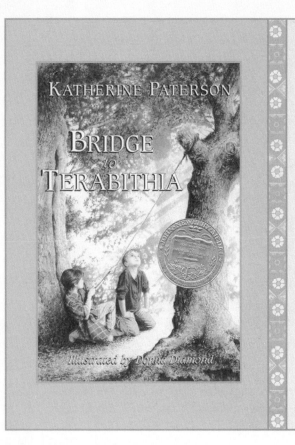

45

Bridge to Terabithia

BY KATHERINE PATERSON

Illustrated by Donna Diamond

144 pages, 2 to 3 hours of reading time
Ages 9 to 12

THEMES
*courage, imagination, friendship,
understanding, encouragement, loss*

The Story

What could be worse than losing the school footrace to a girl? Not much, especially if you are a ten-year-old boy and you've been getting up at the crack of dawn all summer to practice out in the cow pasture. Jess had been living for the moment when he would flash across the finish line and show everyone which fifth-grader runs the fastest. Leslie Burke, a girl *and* a newcomer, puts an end to that dream, but Jess can't help but like the feisty tomboy and they become great friends.

Jess has never met anyone like Leslie, or her rich parents, and Leslie feels pretty lost away from the big city. Their friendship gives Jess relief from the intense pressure of his home life, and in Jess Leslie finds a loyal friend. Their lives and their backgrounds are very different but somehow they form a bond that helps them survive bullies and everyday embarrassments. Naming their secret place in the woods Terabithia, they create "a whole secret country" all their own, a safe place to imagine a bigger, more noble world. One thing they cannot imagine is the tragedy that will strike them and how profoundly life will change. This story is one of yearning and loss and the courage it takes to find healing.

A Page from *Bridge to Terabithia*

For the first time in his life he got up every morning with something to look forward to. Leslie was more than his friend. She was his other, more exciting self— his way to Terabithia and all the worlds beyond.

Terabithia was their secret, which was a good thing, for how could Jess have ever explained it to an outsider? Just walking down the hill toward the woods made something warm and liquid steal through his body. The closer he came to the dry creek bed and the crab apple tree rope the more he could feel the beating of his heart. He grabbed the end of the rope and swung out toward the other bank with a kind of wild exhilaration and landed gently on his feet, taller and stronger and wiser in that mysterious land.

The Heart of the Book

Bridge to Terabithia helps us remember that growing up is not easy. Children face many problems and many of them are serious. Certainly most children feel at times like they have no one to talk to, that they are afraid, that they don't know how to handle their feelings. Often they must grow up too soon, and that is why Terabithia is so important to Jess and Leslie.

✺ *courage*
Jess is afraid of a lot of things, even of being afraid, and he doesn't want anyone, especially Leslie, to know how he feels when these fears rise up in him. The bully at school, the

water in the creek, and the dark pine woods all feel very threatening to him. It is his exercise of courage a little at a time—"I'll just grab that old terror by the shoulders and shake the daylights out of it"—that makes him strong enough to handle terrible catastrophe when it comes.

imagination

"He believed her because there in the shadowy light of the stronghold everything seemed possible." Make-believe is a powerful way for children to experiment with their choices before their character is actually tested in real life. It is true that Jess and Leslie are escaping their circumstances by creating an imaginary world, but they are also giving themselves a safe place to be the courageous and moral people they envision themselves to be.

friendship

In *Bridge to Terabithia*, a lonely boy with a tough father in a house of girls makes friends with a girl who is new in town and not very well accepted. They bring out the best in each other, learn to forgive and to reach out, respect each other, and let each other grow. It is the kind of friendship that is hard to find and cherished forever.

A FEW MORE THINGS TO PONDER . . .

There are many kinds of bridges built in this story. Leslie and Jess help their former enemy, Janice, and are surprised to find that this attempt at *understanding* feels good. Miss Edmunds finds a way to give Jess *encouragement* by acknowledging his artistic talent. Even the terrible *loss* in the story provides a bridge between Jess and his teacher and begins a new connection between the parents and the son.

Reader's Guide

Heads Up *A little bit of extra help*

- Point out where creativity and imagination help Leslie and Jess cope with their difficult circumstances.
- Read to find out how the characters mature as they begin to understand other people and their problems.

- As you read this story, be prepared for the fact that one of the characters will have to deal with the death of someone close to them. These final chapters can evoke a deep emotional response in some readers.
- Notice the realistic portrayal of family relationships.

Dig Deeper   *Some things to think about after you read*

1. Being courageous doesn't mean being unafraid. Name one time Jess shows courage even as he feels fear.
2. Jess loves Miss Edmunds. "He managed to endure the whole boring week of school for that one half hour on Friday afternoons . . ." Why is she important to him?
3. Janice Avery is an enemy at the beginning of the story but becomes Leslie's friend. How does this happen?
4. What are the real threats in Lark Creek, Virginia, where Jess and Leslie live? What are the imaginary dangers in Terabithia?
5. How are words used in a hurtful way in Jess's family?
6. How does his friendship with Leslie make Jess a better person?

- Katherine Paterson's son and his best friend, Lisa, created their own "secret kingdom" when they were young. The author drew from that experience and her son's own tragic loss when she wrote *Bridge to Terabithia*.
- The words "courage" and "encouragement" come from the same Latin word meaning "heart."

46

Miracle's Boys

BY JACQUELINE WOODSON

130 pages, 2 to 3 hours of reading time
Ages 10 to 15

THEMES
*guilt, understanding, loss,
forgiveness, death, family, healing*

The Story

Lafayette sometimes tries to imagine his daddy, but because he never knew him, it is hard. Mama, though, is with him all the time. He lives in a four-room apartment with his older brothers, Ty'ree and Charlie, and since Mama died, nothing has been right.

Twelve-year-old Laf calls his brother Newcharlie because, ever since Charlie came home from the juvenile detention center, he is a different boy than he was before. Now his eyes are cold and he hangs out with the guys in the neighborhood who are up to no good. Charlie is fifteen; if he gets in trouble again, he will go back to doing time and the family will have to split up.

Twenty-one-year-old Ty'ree is doing his best to hold what's left of his family together. A bright young man, he has given up his college dreams to work all day and pinch pennies to make ends meet, and sometimes the bitterness gets the best of him. Each of these boys is carrying a burden of guilt about mistakes he thinks he has made, and they will need the help of a brother to find healing again.

A Page from *Miracle's Boys*

I turned away from both of them and stared out the window. If you ever had a brother who didn't *like* you, then I don't have to explain it. Feels like being a stranger in your own house, like *everything* that used to mean something doesn't anymore. Even your own name. Newcharlie'd hated my guts since Mama died, and he wasn't shy about letting anybody listening know it. Most times when he and Aaron got to talking, I just stayed quiet. If I was real quiet, it was like I was invisible. And if I was invisible, Newcharlie couldn't hate me.

The Heart of the Book

The boys' mother, Milagro (*miracle,* in Spanish), is the glue that holds this family together, and when she is gone, there is a real danger that everything will fall apart. These three sons need one another more than ever.

◉ *guilt*

To Lafayette, it seems that he carries most of the blame for the disintegration of his home. In time, though, he finds out that his brothers walk around with the weight of their own self-imposed guilt. Each one of them must find a way to lay this down.

◉ *understanding*

When Ty'ree tries to explain Charlie to Lafayette, Laf finally sees how helpless and angry Charlie must be. It is the beginning of understanding for him and that is what opens the path toward healing.

✿ loss

This family has lost so much. Milagro lost her husband, her sons lost their dad, and the boys continue to suffer through the death of their mother. Ty'ree feels like he has lost his future, and Charlie has lost himself. Lafayette's anxiety comes from the thought that he might be unable to hold on to the only thing he has left. He is compelled to try to avoid this tragedy.

✿ forgiveness

The only way for Milagro's sons to be whole again is to fully forgive. By opening their hearts and being brave enough to hurt out loud, they will find the strength to forgive themselves and walk toward the future.

A FEW MORE THINGS TO PONDER . . .

These sons are saddened and crippled by Mama's *death*. The story reveals how they learn to deal with it and accept change as a part of life. Charlie turns back to his *family* to help him find his way again, and they find that *healing* is also a natural part of life if they will be open to it.

Reader's Guide

Heads Up   *A little bit of extra help*

- The setting for this story is an inner-city neighborhood.
- Be ready to explain what a juvenile detention center is.
- Be aware that there will be some sad descriptions of the death of family members.

Dig Deeper   *Some things to think about after you read*

1. How does the lack of enough money affect Ty'ree's decisions about his future? How does it affect Charlie?
2. Lafayette likes visiting his Aunt Cecile. Why doesn't he want to live with her?
3. How do Lafayette's dreams reflect his fears?

4. How does Charlie finally see what kind of friend Aaron is?

5. Why is Ty'ree called St. Ty'ree?

6. Describe one important way that Lafayette's memory of his mother influences his decisions.

7. What incident from his past haunts Lafayette? Ty'ree? Charlie?

- A television miniseries was based on *Miracle's Boys*.
- Jacqueline Woodson worked as a drama therapist for runaways and homeless children in New York City.

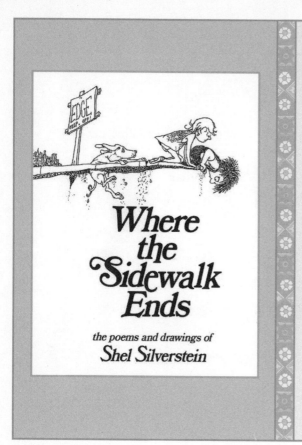

47

Where the Sidewalk Ends

WRITTEN AND
ILLUSTRATED BY
SHEL SILVERSTEIN

Over 120 poems, short to medium-sized
Ages 7 to 11

THEMES
*tolerance, imagination,
creativity, independence*

The Story

Children love to hang out in the magic place where the sidewalk ends. These poems celebrate dancing pants and chickies that refuse to hatch, sing the joys of thumb sucking, and puzzle over what to do with a hippo sandwich.

Some of the verses are only two or three lines long. One or two take up a couple of pages and many are funny enough to get a giggle going. Lots and lots of outrageous fun can be found in these pages, along with a little bit of edgy wisdom.

A Page from *Where the Sidewalk Ends*

POINT OF VIEW

Thanksgiving dinner's sad and thankless
Christmas dinner's dark and blue
When you stop and try to see it
From the turkey's point of view.
Sunday dinner isn't sunny
Easter feasts are just bad luck
When you see it from the viewpoint
Of a chicken or a duck.
Oh how I once loved tuna salad
Pork and lobsters, lamb chops too
Till I stopped and looked at dinner
From the dinner's point of view.

HUG O' WAR

I will not play at tug o' war.
I'd rather play at hug o' war,
Where everyone hugs
Instead of tugs,
Where everyone giggles
And rolls on the rug,
Where everyone kisses,
And everyone grins,
And everyone cuddles,
And everyone wins.

The Heart of the Book

All kids love nonsense, of course, and there is plenty of that in these poems. There are also some good messages to plant in little minds.

⚜ *tolerance*

Some of these poems are a reminder of the great diversity and wonder in the world.

⚜ *imagination*

These little verses are loved because they stretch reality. What fun to imagine a room full of spaghetti or a double-tailed dog.

⚜ *creativity*

The best lesson of all in these poems, whether they are silly or simple, is this: be creative in the way you view the world.

A FEW MORE THINGS TO PONDER . . .

A special kind of *independence* is celebrated in the verse of Shel Silverstein: the freedom to think for oneself.

📖 *Reader's Guide* _____

Heads Up   *A little bit of extra help*

- Notice that the author also illustrated the book. Sometimes his drawing actually completes the poem.
- Make sure you read "With His Mouth Full of Food" out loud.
- Note: Some people find some of the slang and subject matter objectionable in this book. A quick read-through by the adult might be helpful in determining its appropriateness.

Dig Deeper *Some things to think about after you read*

1. Which poems did you like the best?
2. Which ones made you laugh?
3. Did you think the author's pictures fit the poems? Which pictures helped you understand the poem better?
4. How many of the poems are about food?
5. Some of these poems don't rhyme. Why are they still poetry?
6. Put a dollar bill, two quarters, three dimes, four nickels, and five pennies in front of you and then read the poem "Smart." How much money did the son lose?

- *Where the Sidewalk Ends* is one of the best-selling children's poetry books ever. More than four and a half million copies of it have been sold.
- Shel Silverstein wrote Johnny Cash's number-one hit "A Boy Named Sue" in 1969. In 1984, he won a Grammy for his recording of *Where the Sidewalk Ends*.

48.

Homeless Bird

BY GLORIA WHELAN

200 pages, 3 to 4 hours of reading time
Ages 10 to 14

THEMES
*loss, living with uncertainty, love,
abandonment, independence, self-esteem*

The Story

In India, it is not unusual for the parents of a very young girl to arrange their daughter's marriage. When Koly learns that her parents have found a "suitable husband" for her, she is not surprised. She is thirteen, the age at which Indian girls are expected to no longer be a burden to their families. She is eager to meet her new family, but she can't help but be anxious and fearful about leaving home. Soon she finds that she has more reason to despair than she could have ever dreamed. Her husband is only sixteen and is very ill. Her new in-laws have tricked her parents into sending a dowry they cannot afford in order to pay for a trip to dip their son in a sacred river. Soon Koly finds herself a widow at thirteen with no way to go back home, trapped inside a sad, cruel life with a mother-in-law who hates her.

She settles in to make the best of her situation, knowing that her widow's pension check is being stolen from her every month and that she has not one friend to help her. When her mother-in-law abandons her in a huge, unfamiliar city, Koly's own persistence and courage save her from a hopeless existence. With natural talent, the skill of embroidery she learned as a child, and a determination to find her own way, she creates a new life of love and independence.

A Page from *Homeless Bird*

"Koly, you are thirteen and growing every day," Maa said to me. "It's time for you to have a husband." I knew why. There were days when my maa took only a bit of rice for herself so that the rest of us—my baap, my brothers, and I—might have more. "It's one of my days to fast," she would say, as if it were a holy thing, but I knew it was because there was not enough food to go around. The day I left home, there would be a little more for everyone else. I had known the day was coming, but the regret I saw in Maa's eyes made me tremble.

My baap, like all fathers with a daughter to marry off, had to find a dowry for me. "It will be no easy task," he said with a sigh. Baap was a scribe. He sat all day in his marketplace stall hoping to make a few rupees by writing letters for those who did not know how to write their own. His customers had little money. Often from the goodness of his heart Baap would write the letter for only a rupee or two. When I was a small girl, he would sometimes let me stand beside him. I watched as the spoken words were written down to become like caged birds, caught forever by my clever baap.

The Heart of the Book

Koly lives with the reality of limitations. As a child she is not allowed to learn to read because she is a girl. In her new home, she is restricted severely by her role as a widow and by poverty. Because she is so young, she is prevented from making her own choices. Overcoming all of these obstacles, she finds her way to beginning a rich life.

⊛ *loss*

Koly must learn to deal with loss at every turn—the loss of the people she loves, of her own position as a new wife, of her new "sister," Chandra, and of her father-in-law. She is able to translate this loss into beauty with embroidery and learns to use memories and lessons of the past as precious threads as well, making them a permanent part of her soul.

⊛ *living with uncertainty*

In such extreme poverty, the characters in the story live with uncertainty as a constant part of life. Koly's stepmother deals with this reality using deception and dishonesty. Koly, while recognizing those same possibilities within herself, chooses to be hopeful and persevere.

⊛ *love*

In spite of the loss and uncertainty in her life, Koly continues to express and respond to love. She never loses the affection she feels for her family, and her love for Chandra and Tanu is what gives her strength during her most difficult days. It is Raji's devotion to her that will transform the course of Koly's life.

A FEW MORE THINGS TO PONDER . . .

Loneliness and a feeling of *abandonment* are tangible parts of Koly's ordeal. She is left in a miserable home with people who do not love her, eventually losing the only friends she has, and is finally dumped in a city to fend for herself. It is this abandonment, however, that forces her to find her own *independence* and makes her sure of the path she chooses.

Even as she looks ahead with eager anticipation to her new life with Raji, she does so with a new *self-esteem* that comes from having overcome her tragic circumstances.

📖 Reader's Guide _____

Heads Up *A little bit of extra help*

- Note the differences in the culture of India and the culture of the United States concerning young girls and widows.
- Watch for the use of birds as a symbol in the story.
- It might be helpful to read the glossary of common Indian words at the end of the book before you start the story.
- Note the consistent use of threads, embroidery, and quilts as images of how Koly deals with loss and succeeds in surviving.

Dig Deeper *Some things to think about after you read*

1. It is often hard to see the good side of bad events. Koly becomes a widow, trades her silver earrings, and is abandoned in the big city. How were these things positive as well as negative?
2. How does learning to read affect Koly's life?
3. What could be the advantages in arranged marriages?
4. Women have a very restricted place in Indian society, but a very important place in this story. How do the women in *Homeless Bird* react to their social status in different ways?
5. What is a dowry?
6. Why does Koly relate to birds?
7. Who is the person most responsible for Koly's survival and new life?

Koly and her new family travel to Varanasi, the city most sacred to all Hindus. Their belief is that dying in this holy city circumvents reincarnation and assures a permanent place in the Swarg, or heaven.

49.

James and the Giant Peach

BY ROALD DAHL

145 pages, 2 to 3 hours of reading time
Ages 9 to 12

THEMES
*fear, resourcefulness, trust,
loneliness, courage, friendship*

The Story

On a very clear day, James Henry Trotter can see the blue line of the ocean on the horizon. Years ago, he lived by the sea with his loving parents, but now he is an orphan who lives on the top of a very high hill in an old, unfriendly house with his cruel and lazy aunts. They treat him like a slave, calling him ugly names and beating him for no good reason. How James longs to run down off this terrible hill and play by the sea with friends. Aunt Sponge and Aunt Spiker keep a close eye on him, however, and it looks as though he will be trapped in their hateful house forever.

Out of nowhere, a little bald-headed, bristly-bearded old man appears in the garden and offers James a bag of tiny magic crystals. James trips and falls, spilling the crystals underneath the dried-up peach tree, and that's when the adventure begins.

James Henry Trotter is faced with one huge problem after another as he takes a ride in the giant peach with his new friends, Old-Green-Grasshopper, Ladybug, Spider, Glow-Worm, Centipede, Earthworm, and Silkworm. His levelheaded thinking saves them all and lands them in a fantastic new life they could never have imagined.

A Page from *James and the Giant Peach*

"Here we go!" shouted the Old-Green-Grasshopper, hopping up and down with excitement. "Hold on tight!"

"What's happening?" cried James, leaping out of his hammock. "What's going on?"

The Ladybug, who was obviously a kind and gentle creature, came over and stood beside him. "In case you don't know it," she said, "we are about to depart forever from the top of this ghastly hill that we've all been living on for so long. We are about to roll away inside this great big beautiful peach to a land of . . . of . . . of . . . to a land of—"

"Of what?" asked James.

The Heart of the Book

Every new turn of events in *James and the Giant Peach* is a surprise, as the author uses fantasy to take the reader on an exciting ride. Even though most of the characters are overgrown insects, there are some very human lessons here.

✹ *fear*

James is "too frightened to move" when he meets the little old man, but he overcomes his fear and takes the bag of magic crystals. He becomes bolder and bolder as the story goes on, as do the other characters. They find that they can overcome huge problems if they face them squarely.

✹ resourcefulness

Silkworm and Spider spin the answer to the crew's shark problem. Earthworm uses his natural attractiveness to lure the seagulls. Along the way, James learns how each of the creatures is remarkably useful as a resource to the earth.

✹ trust

James has never been able to trust anyone before, but now he has friends who do their best to take care of him, and he does the same for them. His outrageous plans make them all pull together to escape every difficulty.

✹ loneliness

Life with the awful aunts might have been more bearable if James had been able to share his troubles with a friend. Being all alone made him "sadder and sadder, and more and more lonely" as the days went by, and made him even more delighted to find such good friends inside the peach.

A FEW MORE THINGS TO PONDER . . .

While some of the others despaired when survival looked impossible, James found the *courage* to come up with a plan and be the leader. The little boy and his unlikely bug buddies find true *friendship* during their adventures and stay friends after they settle down in their new homes.

📖 Reader's Guide _____

Heads Up *A little bit of extra help*

- Keep a dictionary handy. Dahl uses some interesting words.
- There are lots of great limericks and poems included in *James and the Giant Peach*. Consider reading it aloud.

- Note: The aunts are truly mean in this story and their demise is celebrated. This bothers some readers, as do the insults of the Centipede.
- The author is British, so some of the idioms might be unfamiliar.

Dig Deeper *Some things to think about after you read*

1. Aunt Sponge and Aunt Spiker dislike James. How do they feel about each other?
2. What were the Cloud-Men making out of handfuls of clouds?
3. Why couldn't the sharks eat the peach while it was floating in the ocean?
4. What was one thing James was afraid of? How did he overcome that fear?
5. How does James save Centipede?
6. The people of New York City are afraid when they see the huge insects on the peach. What convinces them that they are harmless?

- A glowworm is a larva of a firefly. Chemicals in the abdomen of the larva are what cause it to glow.
- The Empire State Building is in New York City. It is 102 stories high with a tall lightning rod on the top. Five states can be seen from its top deck.

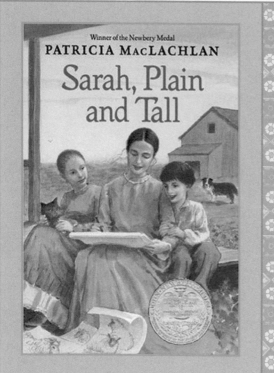

50

Sarah, Plain and Tall

BY PATRICIA MACLACHLAN

64 pages, 1 to 2 hours of reading time
Ages 7 to 12

THEMES
hope, abandonment, family, choice,
nature, work, loneliness, love

The Story

Papa doesn't sing anymore since Mama died, and Anna, his young daughter, tries to explain this to her little brother. Caleb never knew Mama, but he misses her just the same, and all three of the Wittigs feel her absence every day.

Nevertheless, it has been several years and life must go on. Papa needs a wife and the children need a mother, so Joseph Wittig places an ad in the newspaper for a bride. An answer comes all the way from the eastern seaboard to their farm on the plains. Sarah Elizabeth Wheaton writes that she is willing to learn more about them, and after several letters back and forth she agrees to come visit for a month, "just to see," says Papa.

As they all get to know one another, love grows, but so do fear and insecurity. Anna knows that Sarah misses the sea. Caleb is afraid he is too "loud and pesky." They are all aware that she might choose to leave them after all. Anna, Caleb, and Jacob yearn for Sarah to come and fill the loneliness in their little home, but they must wait to find out if this is the choice she will make.

A Page from *Sarah, Plain and Tall*

Sarah turned and looked out over the plains.

"No," she said. "There is no sea here. But the land rolls a little like the sea."

My father did not see her look, but I did. And I knew that Caleb had seen it, too. Sarah was not smiling. Sarah was already lonely. In a month's time the preacher might come to marry Sarah and Papa. And a month was a long time. Time enough for her to change her mind and leave us. Papa took Sarah's bags inside where her room was ready with a quilt on the bed and blue flax dried in a vase on the night table.

Seal stretched and made a small cat sound. I watched her circle the dogs and sniff the air. Caleb came out and stood beside me.

"When will we sing?" he whispered.

I shook my head, turning the white stone over and over in my hand. I wished everything was as perfect as the stone. I wished that Papa and Caleb and I were perfect for Sarah. I wished we had a sea of our own.

The Heart of the Book

This is a straightforward story about a simple event in a family's life but it explores complex feelings. It is about the very basic need for belonging and the desire to be loved.

✸ *hope*

From the moment Papa tells the children about his ad in the paper, their hope begins to grow. Sarah's letters to the Wittigs hold timid suggestions that she wants to find a family, too.

This hope drives all of them to reach out for love and to believe that they can make a good life together.

☸ *abandonment*

Caleb has never had a mother and Anna has been motherless for a long time. In her absence, the children must not only carry more of the weight of the work on the farm, but also cope with their grief and loneliness at the loss of their mother. When Sarah comes for a trial visit, their fear of her departure is more intense because they have been without a mother for so long.

☸ *family*

Anna hurts for her father, and even though she battles resentment against her little brother because her mother died after giving birth to him, she loves him and protects him from her feelings. In this gentle story, the family is strong in spite of tragedy. Sarah fits beautifully into their home because she is willing to love them and be completely involved in her new family's life.

☸ *choice*

Sarah's presence in the Wittig household is much sweeter because she has chosen to stay. She has not promised to, and she does not make the choice lightly, but demonstrates by going into town alone that she has the ability to leave. They know that she loves them more than the life she has left behind. "I will always miss my old home, but the truth of it is I would miss you more."

A FEW MORE THINGS TO PONDER . . .
The children begin to see the world around them with new eyes as Sarah describes her home by the sea and points out the beauty of the *nature* of the plains. The stark landscape and the *work* involved in running a farm contribute to the *loneliness* of the little family before Sarah arrives, while the *love* she exhibits with her generous and willing spirit helps to heal their souls.

Reader's Guide

Heads Up   *A little bit of extra help*

- Take a look at a map of the United States to help picture how far it is from Maine to the Great Plains.
- Notice the ways the author describes the feeling of hope in each character.
- Point out how the author uses color to make the reader see each scene in nature.
- Watch for the use of silence or body language to portray feelings.

Dig Deeper   *Some things to think about after you read*

1. Anna seems very mature for a young girl. Why is this so?
2. What is the first indication that Papa is beginning to feel hopeful?
3. How does Sarah bring the memory of the sea to the farm?
4. Why do the children hope that Sarah can sing?
5. Why is it necessary for Papa to tie a rope from the barn to the house?
6. Sarah obviously feels comfortable doing hard work. How does she show this?
7. Why is it important for Sarah to go to town by herself?

- The author built this story around a real situation from her mother's family history.
- The name of the shell (conch) Sarah brings with her is pronounced "konk" and is used as a trumpet in some cultures.

Ramona takes on fourth grade!

51.

Ramona (series)

BY BEVERLY CLEARY

180 to 190 pages each,
2 to 3 hours of reading time
Ages 7 to 12

THEMES
*family, fear, imagination, friendship,
growing up, compassion, patience*

The Story

Why is life so complicated? Ramona Quimby tries very hard to do the right thing, at least most of the time, but it seems as if problems keep popping up. Admittedly, some of them are her own doing. A panic breaks out at her house when she invites the whole class for a party without telling her mother. A new meaning for the name Egghead is found when she accidentally cracks a raw egg on her head. Most of her troubles are the regular kind, though, like getting along with Danny—Yard Ape, as she likes to call him—or being anxious because of her family's money problems.

As she grows from a four-year-old to a ten-year-old, Ramona wrestles with all of the worries of childhood. She finds out that kids can be mean, parents can make mistakes, and grown-ups are sometimes hard to figure out. She also learns that the world doesn't end when you get sick all over the floor in class, that being the middle child can be a good thing, and that the best kind of family is the one that sticks together—especially when life gets tough.

A Page from *Ramona and Her Mother*

Ramona stopped twirling, staggered from dizziness, and made a face. Willa Jean, the messy little sister of her friend Howie Kemp, was sticky, crumby, into everything, and always had to have her own way.

"And behave yourself," said Mr. Quimby. "Willa Jean is company."

Not my company, thought Ramona, who saw quite enough of Willa Jean when she played at Howie's house. "If Howie can't come to the brunch because he has a cold, why can't Willa Jean stay home with their grandmother, too?" Ramona asked.

"I really don't know," said Ramona's mother. "That isn't the way things worked out. When the Kemps asked if they could bring Willa Jean, I could hardly say no."

I could, thought Ramona, deciding that since Willa Jean, welcome or not, was coming to the brunch, she had better prepare to defend her possessions. She went to her room, where she swept her best crayons and drawing paper into a drawer and covered them with her pajamas.

The Heart of the Book

Following Ramona from kindergarten through elementary school gives the reader a very detailed look into the excitement and anxieties associated with everyday life for a child. Ramona's way of thinking is amusing and familiar to kids and, at the same time, a helpful reminder to adults.

✸ family

Ramona's family has financial problems, employment difficulties, and arguments around the dinner table. They have fun together but they also have emotional disagreements. Ramona worries about all the things that go wrong, and feels secure when problems are solved. She counts on her family to be the solidity in her life.

● *fear*

Every stage of growing up is exciting for Ramona, but she is also filled with big and little fears. Going to a new school gives her "that quivery feeling of excitement in her stomach," but it is complicated by the worry that the bus might make her sick. She likes the idea that her new teachers won't compare her to her big sister, but is concerned that she'll be all alone in a new situation. These stories comfort by saying that fear is normal for all children.

● *imagination*

Ramona is a handful, for sure. Her inventive mind naturally goes toward creative solutions to problems, and she often imagines the worst. Her imagination is also what gives her the ability to learn quickly and makes her such a fun character.

● *friendship*

There is nothing like the friendships of childhood, and Ramona is lucky enough to have several good pals. They have a lot of fun together. Sometimes she finds herself at odds with them, but learns how to forgive and forget. She also has the example of her parents, who usually maintain a warm companionship. Her mother's relationship with her sister, Ramona's Aunt Beatrice, is also a good one. This hints to her that perhaps her connection with her own sister might grow into an adult friendship.

● *growing up*

Ramona bounces through her ordinary life and the reader has the opportunity to see the world through her eyes. She is first a kindergartner and the baby of the family, then a gangly kid who gets in trouble. Finally she is almost ten: a new big sister and much wiser. As she grows, she holds on to her unique outlook, getting better at making decisions and understanding the grown-up world around her.

A FEW MORE THINGS TO PONDER . . .
Ramona sometimes struggles with feeling "mean and unhappy" and she knows, like everyone, that she has a "dark, deep-down place inside her" that won't always let her do the

right thing, but her intense thoughts lead her to *compassion* for others, like pretty, perfect Susan, who has problems of her own. In turn, this teaches Ramona *patience,* because she sees that her first idea may not always be the best idea.

Reader's Guide

Heads Up *A little bit of extra help*

- The first book in this series is *Beezus and Ramona*.
- These books are especially fun for girls, but boys like them, too.

Dig Deeper *Some things to think about after you read*

1. What does Ramona do with the apples in *Beezus and Ramona*? How does her mother make the best of the situation?
2. In *Ramona and Her Father*, how do Beezus and Ramona think they are going to save Mr. Quimby's life?
3. What is Beezus's given name?
4. Why does Ramona "sort of like" Danny after she gets her eraser back in *Ramona Quimby, Age 8*?
5. What does "D.E.A.R" stand for?
6. In *Ramona's World*, why does Ramona make a face in her school photo?
7. Mrs. Quimby decides that her daughters can stay at home after school by themselves in *Ramona Forever*. Why?

The Beverly Cleary Sculpture Garden for Children, featuring bronze statues of the book characters Ramona Quimby, Henry Huggins, and Ribsy, was built in the author's honor in Portland, Oregon.

52

A Wrinkle in Time

BY MADELEINE L'ENGLE

240 pages, 4 to 5 hours of reading time
Ages 8 to 13

THEMES
*individuality, first impressions, living with
uncertainty, love, flaws, responsibility*

The Story

Meg Murry has the same troubles as most high school girls. She feels awkward and unpretty, and has lately been getting into a good bit of trouble at school.

There may be a good reason for this, though: she is worried about her father, who has been missing for an entire year.

One stormy night, Meg's mother brings in from the rain an old woman who looks like a tramp. Soon the family discovers that the woman and her two friends are living in an old, abandoned house nearby and are not old women at all. They are actually otherworldly creatures in human form. They shock Meg and her companions with information about the plight of Meg's father and give warning of a terrifying threat to the universe. The three children are transported through time and space on a mission to rescue Meg's father, who is held in the grip of an evil force.

In a tale that spins from earth to Camazotz, a far-off planet engulfed by the Dark Thing, to Ixchel, the gray world of furry beasts, Meg and her companions confront pure evil and discover the truth about the supernatural power of love.

A Page from *A Wrinkle in Time*

"Now, don't be frightened, loves," Mrs. Whatsit said. Her plump little body began to shimmer, to quiver, to shift. The wild colors of her clothes became muted, whitened.

The pudding-bag shape stretched, lengthened, merged. And suddenly before the children was a creature more beautiful than any Meg had even imagined, and the beauty lay in far more than the outward description. Outwardly Mrs. Whatsit was surely no longer a Mrs. Whatsit. She was a marble-white body with powerful flanks, something like a horse but at the same time completely unlike a horse, for from the magnificently modeled back sprang a nobly formed torso, arms, and a head resembling a man's, but a man with a perfection of dignity and virtue, an exaltation of joy such as Meg had never before seen. No, she thought, it's not like a Greek centaur. Not in the least.

From the shoulders slowly a pair of wings unfolded, wings made of rainbows, of light upon water, of poetry.

Calvin fell to his knees.

"No," Mrs. Whatsit said, though her voice was not Mrs. Whatsit's voice. "Not to me, Calvin. Never to me. Stand up."

The Heart of the Book

A Wrinkle in Time grabs the imagination of young readers. Behind the story there are powerful cosmic concepts—the battle between good and evil, time travel, and the possibilities of supernatural communication. The book is spiced with plenty of creepy creatures and exciting surprises, and tucked into the pages are many valuable insights for children.

⚜ *individuality*

Meg is at war with herself. She hates how she looks and she feels like an outsider. She just wants to fit in and be like everyone else. When she lands on a planet of identical houses and identical people, she is jolted into the realization that there is great value in our unique differences and creativity, and there is the possibility of great harm in conformity. Meg learns appreciation for individuality, especially her own. "Maybe I don't like being different, but I don't want to be like everybody else, either." She is given one of the most valuable gifts a child can receive—the knowledge that she is one of a kind, an original.

⚜ *first impressions*

Many people around the Murry family think Charles Wallace, Meg's little brother, is not very smart, but his family knows that he has very special gifts indeed. Mrs. Whatsit, Mrs. Who, and Mrs. Which are certainly not old ladies but instead creatures from another world, and the place on Camazotz that looks the most ordinary of all is the most sinister. That's how Meg and her buddies find out that first impressions can be deceiving. Better to let time and experience show what is true.

⚜ *living with uncertainty*

Most children, like Meg in this story, have a lot of questions. Meg wants answers and is impatient when her questions are left unexplained. But when she is forced into a confrontation with the giant pulsating brain called IT, she sees the danger of a mind that requires such exact explanations and she begins to push against that force. Meg learns that sometimes she must accept that there are going to be things she doesn't understand. She begins to find her own courage in the face of uncertainty.

A FEW MORE THINGS TO PONDER . . .

Other larger, more universal ideas fuel this book's story. The Murry family finds out that the power of *love* is stronger than the Black Thing. Love can be communicated without words. It is their bond and it is the power that ultimately defeats the darkness of evil. Meg also learns that her *flaws* can be turned into strength, that love is expressed not only with words but also with actions, and that growing up means taking personal *responsibility* in doing good.

Reader's Guide

Heads Up

- This book is a good example of science fiction for young readers, but it can also be considered a fantasy story.
- The plot of this story is built around the discovery of a "tesseract." Use a dictionary to discover the definition before you read.
- Encourage your child to draw pictures of some of the extraordinary characters described in *A Wrinkle in Time*.

Dig Deeper   *Some things to think about after you read*

1. As the story begins, how do we know that Meg feels like she doesn't fit in at school?
2. What does she learn on Camazotz that helps her feel differently about that?
3. The awesome power of love binds this family and saves the universe. When exactly does that power take effect?
4. It's sometimes hard to wait for answers. What are some answers that Meg had to wait for?
5. What saves Charles Wallace from the power of IT?
6. In this story, which characters are not what they seem?
7. Point out the wrong first impressions, and the right ones.

- This book is the first in Madeleine L'Engle's Time quartet, which includes *A Wrinkle in Time*, *A Wind in the Door*, *A Swiftly Tilting Planet*, and *Many Waters*.
- Madeleine L'Engle brings her Christian point of view to this book. The characters are not shown in any sort of formal church settings, but Scripture is quoted, and Jesus Christ is used as a positive example.

53.

My Side of the Mountain

BY
JEAN CRAIGHEAD GEORGE

175 pages, 3 to 4 hours of reading time
Ages 9 to 12

THEMES
*self-sufficiency, nature, resourcefulness,
loneliness, confidence, friendship*

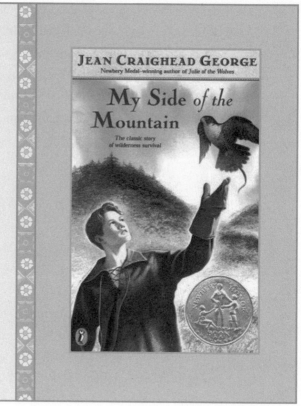

The Story

As fifteen-year-old Sam Gribley sat in the hollowed-out ancient hemlock tree he lived in, he thought about the tiny apartment he had shared with his parents and eight brothers and sisters. He was many miles and many months away from New York City and he was getting used to being alone. Sam had run away to the wild country in the Catskill Mountains, to land that had belonged to his great-grandfather Gribley, carrying only a penknife, a ball of cord, an ax, forty dollars, and some flint and steel. He has thrived out in the wilderness, loving the solitude and his independence.

As Sam tells the story of his year on the mountain, he recounts his fears and failures, and the thrill of discovering his own ability to do absolutely everything for himself. What does a young man do when he realizes that he is going to need warmer clothes for winter? How can he boil water without a pot? Is it possible to capture a baby falcon and train it to hunt? Sam uses all the knowledge he has soaked up from library books and experts he has met along the way. He makes his dream of living with nature come true, raises Frightful the falcon to hunt for him, and learns much about our basic human longing for companionship.

A Page from *My Side of the Mountain*

Frightful flapped. I held her wings to her body as her flapping was noisy to me. Apparently not so to the man. The man did not stir. It is hard to realize that the rustle of a falcon's wings is not much of a noise to a man from the city, because by now, one beat of her wings and I would awaken from a sound sleep as if a shot had gone off. The stranger slept on. I realized how long I'd been in the mountains.

Right at that moment, as I looked at his unshaven face, his close-cropped hair, and his torn clothes, I thought of the police siren, and put two and two together.

"An outlaw!" I said to myself. "Wow!" I had to think what to do with an outlaw before I awoke him.

The Heart of the Book

It is often a boy's dream to leave civilization behind and escape to the woods, to prove himself capable of survival. *My Side of the Mountain* is essentially the diary of a young man who does exactly that.

⚙ *self-sufficiency*

Jean Craighead George's father was a naturalist and scientist who taught his young daughter how to find sustenance in woods and rivers. This book is a manual for living off the land and is filled with fascinating details about trapping, fishing, and finding edible plants.

⚙ *nature*

"Spring is terribly exciting when you are living right in it." Sam finds that it is not only possible to live by himself in the woods, it is a life that is peaceful and joyful. Nature is almost always communicative, if he will only listen.

⚙ *resourcefulness*

Sam has none of the things that are taken for granted in everyday life. He has no fishhook, no bucket, no lamp. He begins to see the world around him in a different way and to discover his own creativity as he looks for answers to his needs.

⚙ *loneliness*

His days are filled with activity and usually he feels safe and fed, but Sam finds that he needs human company. As his loneliness grows, he begins to seek out companionship rather than hide from it and finally chooses to welcome his family into his world.

A FEW MORE THINGS TO PONDER . . .

Sam is determined to follow through with his mission, and his **confidence** grows stronger as he learns to survive in the wild. He develops a ***friendship*** with the falcon and the weasel, but it is his relationships with the boys in town and with his family that become more important to him.

✎ Reader's Guide _____

Heads Up *A little bit of extra help*

- Find a picture of a neighborhood in New York City and compare it with a photograph of the Catskill Mountains.
- Keep an encyclopedia nearby for looking up pictures of the animals in the story.
- Read the author's introduction to the book. It explains why she could write this story in such a believable style.

Dig Deeper *Some things to think about after you read*

1. Why don't Sam's parents find him and bring him home?
2. What are some of the major dangers Sam faces?
3. How does Sam's appetite tell him he is missing some nutrients?
4. Is Sam wise when he decides to hide Bando, whom he thinks is an outlaw?
5. *My Side of the Mountain* is set in the 1950s. How might Sam's reaction to intruders have been different today?
6. What is the story behind the name Gribley's Folly?
7. Sam has mixed feelings about his family coming to the mountain. Why?

- Peregrine falcons are said to be the fastest birds on earth, because their diving speed can be over 200 miles per hour.
- In the 1940s, Jean Craighead George was a reporter for the *Washington Post* and a member of the White House Press Corps.

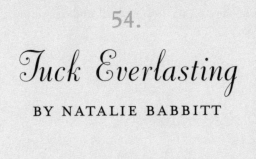

54.

Tuck Everlasting

BY NATALIE BABBITT

144 pages, 2 to 3 hours of reading time
Ages 9 to 13

THEMES
*coming of age, death, freedom,
honesty, passage of time, mortality*

The Story

It is a miserably hot August. Winnie Foster sits looking through the bars of the fence around her house and wishes for freedom. "I expect I'd better run away," she says, exasperated and bored with her ten-year-old life with all of its rules and limitations. When the sound of a lovely melody lures her into the woods, she happens upon a young man taking a drink from a spring under a huge tree and her life-changing adventure begins.

The young man is Jesse Tuck, one of the two sons of Mae and Angus Tuck, and he is seventeen years old—sort of. What Winnie finds out after the Tucks kidnap her and take her to their cabin is that this family stopped growing older eighty-seven years ago, when they first drank from the magic spring. They hope to convince Winnie to keep their secret, believing that the revelation of this knowledge would mean disaster. A mysterious man hovers nearby, wanting the spring for his own greedy purposes, and in a sudden turn, Mae Tuck is compelled to extreme measures in an effort to hide this fountain of eternal life from the rest of the world.

Winnie is young but she must make some grown-up decisions. As she tries to do the right thing for herself and for the people she loves, she takes a step toward understanding the beauty and fragility of life.

A Page from *Tuck Everlasting*

"It goes on," Tuck repeated, "to the ocean. But this rowboat now, it's stuck. If we didn't move it out ourself, it would stay here forever, trying to get loose, but stuck. That's what us Tucks are, Winnie. Stuck so's we can't move on. We ain't part of the wheel no more. Dropped off, Winnie. Left behind. And everywhere around us, things is moving and growing and changing. You, for instance. A child now, but someday a woman. And after that, moving on to make room for the new children."

Winnie blinked, and all at once her mind was drowned with understanding of what he was saying.

The Heart of the Book

Winnie finds herself in a world in which immortality is an option, and her view of life is tested.

⚙ *coming of age*
To protect her new friends, Winnie makes hard decisions. She must process all of the new fantastic information she has been given and choose a path all by herself, and this is a major step toward maturity.

⚙ *death*
Angus Tuck watches the dying man "as if he were entranced," because he is envious. If death is seen as part of the natural cycle of life, it can be welcomed at the right time.

✪ freedom

In one sense, the Tucks are free to do whatever they want to because they cannot die. Winnie, on the other hand, feels trapped in her boring life. However, it is the Tuck family whose life is limited eternally and Winnie who finds her life is one to be cherished.

✪ honesty

Winnie has to deceive her family, lie to the constable, and break the law in order to protect the secret and save her friends. She will have to find out for herself if this was the right thing to do.

A FEW MORE THINGS TO PONDER . . .

The Tucks live day after day with no hope of the natural rhythm of change and growth that comes with the gift of the *passage of time*. They long for *mortality,* seeing it as a blessing, not a curse.

Reader's Guide

Heads Up *A little bit of extra help*

- This story is about the natural circle of life. Notice the many wheel symbols.
- Look for the use of contrasts in *Tuck Everlasting*: hot and cold, wet and dry, limits and freedom. These can be seen as pictures of the choices Winnie must make.

Dig Deeper *Some things to think about after you read*

1. Why does Winnie wish for a sister or a brother?
2. Why do the Tucks have to keep moving?
3. How does the stranger in the yellow suit plan to get ownership of the woods and the spring?
4. Mae was guilty of what crime? Why is it important that she not be convicted?
5. How does Winnie feel about being deceitful to her parents?

6. Why does Tuck say that he would gladly "climb back on the wheel" if he knew how?

7. How does the reality of death make us live life differently?

- In Norse mythology, Yggdrasil, also called the World Tree, is a giant ash tree that links and shelters the world. At its base are the Well of Wisdom, the Well of Fate, and the Roaring Kettle, the source of many rivers.

- An ancient legend says that Alexander the Great traveled to the top of the world and there found the Land of Darkness. In that land, his servant drank from the Water of Life and became immortal.

Special Comfort Books

55

The Story About Ping

BY MARJORIE FLACK
AND KURT WIESE

32 pages, 10 minutes of reading time
Ages 2 to 6

THEMES
*fear, prudence, abandonment,
responsibility, obedience, courage*

The Story

Ping had a happy life on the riverboat with his large family and his kind master. They floated on the river at night, and by day pecked and played and looked for nice things to eat. When it was time to go back home in the evening, Ping knew not to be the last duck to board the riverboat because that meant a spanking. When he finds himself the last one in line one day, he hides in the tall grass to avoid the consequences. That leaves him all alone the next morning with the whole Yangtze River in front of him, facing the task of finding his family. After being captured and then escaping an almost certain fate in the cookpot, Ping learns that it is always better to face up to discipline than to try to hide from it.

A Page from *The Story About Ping*

"Ah, a duck dinner has come to us!" said the Boy's father.

"I will cook him with rice at sunset tonight," said the Boy's mother.

"NO-NO! My nice duck is too beautiful to eat," cried the Boy.

But down came a basket all over Ping and he could see no more of the Boy or the boat or the sky or the beautiful yellow water of the Yangtze river.

The Heart of the Book

This classic story remains a favorite because all children relate to the feelings of the little duck.

❀ *fear*

Ping is very afraid of punishment and he soon finds that there are more things in the big world to be afraid of.

❀ *prudence*

Ping learns a hard first lesson in using good sense.

❀ *abandonment*

The scary feeling of being left alone is a universal one for children. Ping wants desperately to be back with his happy family.

❀ *responsibility*

Being the last one to board the boat is Ping's fault, and a first step in growing up is learning to be accountable for his actions.

A FEW MORE THINGS TO PONDER . . .

By having an almost disastrous foray on his own, Ping learns *obedience* for the rules and that real *courage* is facing up to the consequences of his deeds.

Heads Up   *A little bit of extra help*

- *The Story About Ping* takes place on the Yangtze River in China. Use a globe or a map to show how far away it is.
- In this story, the last duck on board gets a spank. Be ready to explain to the reader that this protected the ducks by insuring that none of them would be late, and that therefore none would be left behind.
- This story might be a comfort to a child who has just been disciplined.

Dig Deeper   *Some things to think about after you read*

1. How many cousins did Ping have?
2. What happened to the last duck to cross over the little bridge to the riverboat? Why?
3. What were some of the things that made Ping afraid while he was alone on the river?
4. The next time Ping finds himself last to cross the bridge, how will he behave differently?

The Yangtze River is the longest river in Asia and the third longest in the world. Only the Amazon and the Nile are longer.

56.

The Tenth Good Thing About Barney

BY JUDITH VIORST

Illustrated by Erik Blegvad

32 pages, 10 minutes of reading time
Ages 5 to 7

THEMES
comfort, gratitude, death, mortality, honesty

The Story

Barney the cat died Friday and on Saturday morning the people who knew him gathered to say good-bye. Losing him was a sad thing, especially for the little boy who loved him most. As he tries to understand, he lists the good things about Barney. It is his father's gentle explanation of the cycle of life that helps him most.

A Page from *The Tenth Good Thing About Barney*

My mother sat down on my bed, and she gave me a hug.

She said we could have a funeral for Barney in the morning.

She said I should think of ten good things about Barney so I could tell them at the funeral.

The Heart of the Book

This straightforward look at the inevitable event of a pet's death will be the right approach for some children.

⚙ *comfort*

His mother's hugs and his father's words, along with the homegrown liturgy of the funeral under the tree, help to soften the boy's loss.

⚙ *gratitude*

The boy remembers Barney with fondness, and thinks of all the good things he brought to his life.

⚙ *death*

The finality of the cat's absence is the main difficulty for the little boy. He wants to know where Barney is but he doesn't like his own answer and he doesn't like Annie's answer, either.

A FEW MORE THINGS TO PONDER . . .

Every living thing has an end to its life on earth. *Mortality* is natural. The father speaks to his son with quiet and simple *honesty* and gives his son a new way to deal with this reality.

Reader's Guide

Heads Up   *A little bit of extra help*

- As with all books about sensitive subjects, the adult should read *The Tenth Good Thing about Barney* to determine if it is appropriate before giving it to a child to read.
- These illustrations evoke different feelings in each reader. Ask about them as you read.

Dig Deeper   *Some things to think about after you read*

1. How do the boy's actions show that he is sad?
2. What does his mother think might make him feel better?
3. Where does Annie think Barney has gone?
4. "That's a pretty nice job for a cat," the boy decides. What does he mean?

Judith Viorst has written books of poetry and fiction for adults and children, and three musicals that are still being performed in theaters.

57.

I Love You, Little One

BY NANCY TAFURI

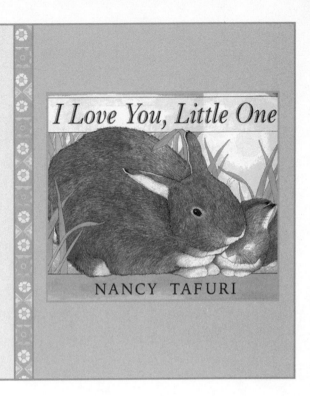

32 pages, 5 to 8 minutes of reading time

Infants to age 5

THEMES
comfort, nature, bedtime, love

The Story

Deep in a lush, mysterious forest and high in a brown oak tree, by the beautiful pond lilies and in the green grass by a sandy riverbank, little animals ask, "Do you love me?" Mama animals nuzzle and reassure, all with the same answer, but uniquely framed for their own child. Night falls and in a log house it is bedtime for a little child. He, too, finds comfort in the words of his mother, who promises to love "forever and ever, and always."

The Heart of the Book

Great for bedtime or any read-aloud time, *I Love You, Little One* gently conveys its positive message.

⚙ *comfort*
The words of each mother in this story and the warm, orderly, detailed paintings echo the reassurance every child needs.

⚙ *nature*
The luxurious size of these pages and the rich attention to every blade of grass and duck feather make the world of nature very appealing.

⚙ *bedtime*

As the reader turns the pages of this beautifully illustrated book, the light changes in each scene and the day progresses from morning to night, until finally the stars are overhead and it is bedtime.

A FEW MORE THINGS TO PONDER . . .

The reader believes in the mama animals' *love*. The tender words are accompanied by closeness and cuddling.

📖 *Reader's Guide*

Heads Up   *A little bit of extra help*

- Notice how Nancy Tafuri creates rhythm and emphasis in her illustrations. We see the little one ask the question in a smaller drawing on the right side of the pages. When the mother answers, the perspective is much closer and intimate. This gives weight to her soothing reply.
- *I Love You, Little One* is a wonderful bedtime book.

Dig Deeper   *Some things to think about after you read*

1. What are some of the different animals in this story?
2. Do the little animals feel better after the mother animals answer the question?
3. How long will the mothers love their little ones?

You Are Special, Little One, also written by Nancy Tafuri, is a celebration of the uniqueness of each child.

Books for Adults Recommended by Laura Bush

Ship of Fools   Katherine Anne Porter

The Collected Stories of Katherine Anne Porter   Katherine Anne Porter

The Brothers Karamazov   Fyodor Dostoyevsky

Beloved   Toni Morrison

Music for Chameleons   Truman Capote

Goodbye to a River   John Graves

Mornings on Horseback and other biographies   David McCullough

Bless Me, Ultima   Rudolfo A. Anaya

My Ántonia   Willa Cather

Death Comes to the Archbishop   Willa Cather

All the Pretty Horses   Cormac McCarthy

The Educational Organizations
Laura Bush Supports

When asked whether she felt obligated to use her clout as First Lady to bring about change, Laura Bush told Jim Lehrer in May 2001 that she thought of her influential public platform instead as "a wonderful opportunity." She went on to say, "The issues that are important to me are what I think are some of the most important issues in our country." Those issues are education and teaching, and this is where she chooses to use her clout most often.

Laura Bush's causes are carefully crafted to complement one another. In one program, reading to toddlers is encouraged; in another, parents are given the tools to help their children learn the basics for school. In yet another initiative, school libraries are given the books they need to guide students toward a joy of learning, while several other programs train teachers in excellence to meet the challenges of the classroom. In all of Mrs. Bush's initiatives, communities come together and parents and teachers join forces in this most important job of all—educating our children.

Most of the programs Laura Bush supports fall into two categories: first, initiatives that deliver proven methods for early childhood training in language development, and second, alternative teacher recruitment programs that call on the energy and experience of individuals from noneducation backgrounds to fill a critical need for teachers in our schools. In addition, she devotes her energy to other projects that support literature and libraries: the National Book Festival, the White House Salute to America's Author series, and the Laura Bush Foundation.

In all of her efforts for promoting literacy, Laura Bush's central vision is the impact a literate society has upon future generations. As she once stated in an article for a parenting magazine: "We must remember that the education we provide our children from the day they are born will shape the way they think and learn. The quality of their education will either drive or stifle the enthusiasm, motivation, and effort they put into learning. It will affect how they interact with others and their ability to adapt to their successes and setbacks throughout their lives."

As is evident from the following annotated list, these values permeate all of Mrs. Bush's causes for education and literature.

1. The White House Summit on Early Childhood Cognitive Development

This two-day gathering of highly respected and innovative researchers in the field of early cognitive development was hosted in July 2001 by Mrs. Bush, along with U.S. Secretary of Education Rod Paige and U.S. Secretary of Health and Human Services Tommy Thompson. Scientists presented research proving that babies seek out language information during the first year of life and made the case that parents and caretakers who take the time and effort to engage children in exciting learning activities help ensure future academic success. By contrast, children who are not engaged in such activities are at risk. Summit speakers stressed the importance of preschool development. G. Reid Lyon from the National Institutes of Health made this statement:

> We have learned that if we do not help our kids get ready for school, the damage to their futures not only reflects an educational problem, but a public health problem as well. Children who do not receive a strong language and emergent literacy foundation during the preschool years frequently have difficulties comprehending and using language and developing strong reading and writing abilities throughout their school tenure. No doubt, this lack of development places these children at later risk for school failure, and for limited occupational and economic success, not to mention detriments to their well-being.

> For more information: whitehouse.gov/firstlady/initiatives/education/earlychildhood.html.

2. Healthy Start, Grow Smart

Mrs. Bush cosponsored the *Healthy Start, Grow Smart* series while she was the First Lady of Texas, and continued her support when she moved into the White House. This collection of free booklets for new parents has been revised and can be found on the Internet at www.ed.gov.

Healthy Start, Grow Smart is available in English and Spanish and includes thirteen brochures, beginning with "Your Newborn" and ending with "Your Twelve-Month-Old." Each booklet is designed to give new parents clear and helpful information on how to give their children an early start toward education.

Babies are born to learn. They naturally want to learn. Research shows that babies can identify the sounds of their own language and the rhythms of words and phrases very early. Because this is the foundation for talking and reading, these early months of development are important ones.

The booklet for newborns includes information on breastfeeding, soothing a crying baby, installing car seats properly, and advice for fathers on changing diapers.

The last booklet in the series, "Your Twelve-Month-Old," lists developmental benchmarks for a child at twelve months and gives information about early intervention if concerns about a child's development arise. Also included are articles about parenting styles, child safety, and age-appropriate games for parents to play with their child.

For more information: ed.gov/parents/earlychild/ready/healthystart/index.html.

3. Ready to Read, Ready to Learn

At the heart of this initiative launched by Laura Bush in February 2001 is this statement from the *Head Start Policy Book*: "Reading scores in the 10th grade can be predicted with surprising accuracy based on a child's knowledge of the alphabet in kindergarten."

This initiative has two major goals. The first is ensuring that all young children are ready to read and learn when they enter their first classroom. The second objective is recruiting qualified teachers and training them well. This goal is especially important for schools in our most impoverished neighborhoods.

As a public school teacher, Mrs. Bush often noticed that some children were having difficulty learning to read. As she commented in January 2002, when she addressed a Senate committee on improving early childhood education, "It was troubling to watch these little ones struggle with print, but it was even more troubling to see how embarrassed and frustrated they were by their failure to do what they saw other children do. It was as if their self-esteem and confidence took a blow every time they tried to read."

A child cannot succeed without language and reading skills. For children to achieve these skills, teachers must be trained in the most effective ways to teach. Moms, dads, older siblings, and grandparents should be convinced that they play an important role in the process. By using fun activities, such as language play, sound games, reading aloud together, and talking about book characters and content, family members can help children be ready to succeed.

For more information: ed.gov/teachers/how/read/rrrl/part.html.

4. The Designated Reader Campaign

On April 3, 2002, the Public Broadcasting System launched a national public service campaign to promote children's literacy. Designated Reader was designed to help millions of children become better readers by inspiring adults to read aloud to them every day. PBS delivers the Designated Reader message by broadcasting public service messages, recruiting local celebrity and role-model readers, and incorporating it into the storylines of its series *Between the Lions*.

"PBS is proud that Mrs. Bush will support this campaign to uplift every child through the priceless gift of reading," said Pat Mitchell, president and CEO of PBS. "I can think of no better voice to call on all Americans to change a life by reading to a child."

For more information: pbs.org/aboutpbs/news/20020403_desreader.html.

5. Get Caught Reading

Get Caught Reading is a literacy campaign supported by the book publishing industry. Prominent American figures, including Laura Bush, Robin Williams, Derek Jeter, Whoopi Goldberg, Rosie O'Donnell, Sammy Sosa, Dolly Parton, Jane Seymour, Jake Lloyd, Clifford the Big Red Dog, Donald Duck, and the Rugrats, are pictured in posters that spread the word that we should all Get Caught Reading.

For more information: getcaughtreading.org.

6. Reach Out And Read

Created by a team of pediatricians in Boston, this program is used in clinics where doctors and nurses give prescriptions for reading as part of regular well-child visits.

During each visit, the child receives a new book and the parent is given instructions on reading to that child every day. Laura Bush initiated Reach Out and Read in Texas in 1997 and helped to open more than sixty programs around that state.

For more information: reachoutandread.org.

7. New Teacher Project

I'm going to encourage more people to bring their talents, energy and enthusiasm to the classroom, especially in schools that need help the most.

LAURA BUSH, ADDRESSING THE HOOVER INSTITUTION, WASHINGTON, D.C., FEBRUARY 2001

The New Teacher Project partners with educational entities to develop programs across the United States to recruit high-achieving individuals who are willing to take on the challenge of teaching in America's classrooms. Since 1997, the nonprofit organization has attracted and trained more than thirteen thousand new teachers, and has discovered that some of the nation's most talented citizens will dedicate themselves to teaching if school districts will give them the opportunity and support they need. Recruits commit to two years of teaching. While teaching full time, they also will pursue master's degrees in education.

For more information: tntp.org.

8. Transition to Teaching

This government program awards grants to a variety of institutions to help them recruit, prepare, and place professionals in teaching careers. U.S. Secretary of Education Rod Paige has expressed high hopes for this program because it streamlines the process of placing qualified educators in high-need school districts: "We must tap the energy, experience, and eagerness of individuals from noneducation backgrounds into the teaching profession."

In a speech about education reform in February 2001, Laura Bush voiced her belief that, through this and other innovative recruitment programs, "we'll meet the national challenge of training and recruiting more teachers over the next decade."

For more information: transitiontoteaching.org.

9. Teach for America

This national corps is composed of outstanding recent college graduates of all academic majors, committed to teaching for two years in urban and rural public schools and becoming leaders in the effort to expand educational opportunity. Currently, 3,500 corps members are teaching in over one thousand schools across the country as part of Teach for America.

Corps members begin their two-year commitment by attending a rigorous summer training institute, where they are taught proven methods used by successful teachers in low-income communities. During their training, they also receive instruction in the six courses that comprise the Teach for America curriculum, teach in a summer school program, and train with experienced educators.

Wendy Kopp, the president and founder of Teach for America, credits Laura Bush with helping the organization succeed. "I truly believe that Laura Bush's support was one of the things that helped catapult us forward." Mrs. Bush appeared at recruiting events in Arizona and the Mississippi Delta, spoke at a national fundraising event in San Francisco, and taught in New York classrooms to bring publicity to the cause.

For more information: teachforamerica.org/flash_movie.html.

10. Troops to Teachers

Laura Bush believes that our schools need to "call in the military!" as she stated in her remarks to the Hoover Institution in 2001. "Retired members of the military protected our nation in war and led the world in peace, and many are well qualified to guide children in school. We need to help tap this respected pool of talent by supporting the Troops to Teachers Program." She went on to comment on this valuable asset, "Many in the Troops to Teachers Program have science, math, and engineering degrees—disciplines that our children desperately need. Beyond that, these men and women are tremendous role models with a sense of duty, honor, and country that our children would do well to emulate."

This program was established by the Department of Defense in 1994, and its goal is to help eligible military personnel begin new careers as teachers in public schools. In 2002, Congress and President Bush reauthorized funds to offer stipends to qualified participants in the program, and Mrs. Bush seeks to enlist more teachers from the ranks of the armed forces when visiting bases around the country.

For more information: proudtoserveagain.com/pages/808014.

11. Texas Book Festival

The year 1996 marked the beginning of what has become a nationally renowned literary event that raises money for Texas libraries. This event was a perfect project for Laura Bush, the book lover, librarian, and Texan.

The Texas Book Festival celebrates authors and their contributions to the culture of literacy, ideas, and imagination, and is held on the grounds of the Texas State Capitol. It is currently the largest private funding source for Texas public libraries, awarding grants that are used to sponsor literacy programs as well as technology projects. This event served as the model for the National Book Festival, an annual celebration of books and reading, held on the lawn of the U.S. Capitol.

For more information: texasbookfestival.org.

12. National Book Festival

The National Book Festival celebrates the joy of America's literary culture. Books tell us the story of who we are as a nation.

LAURA BUSH, ADDRESSING THE FIFTH NATIONAL BOOK FESTIVAL GALA, WASHINGTON, D.C., 2005

Laura Bush joined with the Library of Congress to launch the first National Book Festival in Washington, D.C., in September 2001. The 2004 festival drew 85,000 book lovers from across the nation, with an even larger crowd of ninety thousand in 2005. Many Americans who could not be present at the event watched the discussions via cable telecast and streaming video at public libraries nationwide. Each year, book/author pavilions are available for visits, and dozens of authors and illustrators participate. The 2005 festival featured David McCullogh, E. L. Doctorow, Sue Monk Kidd, John Irving, Linda Sue Park, and journalist Thomas Friedman.

For more information: loc.gov/bookfest.

13. The White House Salute to American Authors

This series of literary events was developed to honor some of America's most significant authors. In each symposium, the literary giants of our past are brought together with the notable writers of today. Scholars, students, and educators gather to discuss the country's important writers and become part of an effort to engage Americans, particularly children, in reading great works.

The first White House Salute to America's Authors included a tribute to the works of Mark Twain. "Few, if any, American writers could turn a phrase better than Mark Twain," said Mrs. Bush in remarks at the event, adding, "Millions of Americans have enjoyed the results, including the president. His favorite quote is, 'Do the right thing. It will gratify a few and amaze the rest.'"

The White House Salute to America's Authors has since celebrated the diverse writers of the Harlem Renaissance, three women writers of the American West (Willa Cather, Edna Ferber, and Laura Ingalls Wilder), and Truman Capote, Flannery O'Connor, and Eudora Welty in its Symposium on Classic American Stories.

For more information: whitehouse.gov/firstlady/initiatives/wh-salute.html.

14. The Laura Bush Foundation

This organization has awarded millions of dollars in grants to help school libraries across the country create or enhance their book collections. Since its creation in 2002, the Laura Bush Foundation has received thousands of applications from elementary, middle, and high schools, both public and private. An award of up to five thousand dollars is granted to each recipient school selected. The Laura Bush Foundation is supported by donations from individuals, corporations, and foundations.

For more information: laurabushfoundation.org.

Index by Theme

Index by Genre

Index by Title
and Author/Illustrator

About the Author

Beverly Darnall has written songs recorded by Eric Clapton, Amy Grant, Vince Gill, and others; has produced live concert tours and DVDs; and has run a music publishing firm. She is executive director of Chartwell Literary Group (www.chartwellliterary.com), a company that creates and manages literary projects. She lives in Nashville.